MY LORDS, LADIES
AND GENTLEMEN

MY LORDS, LADIES AND GENTLEMEN

A guide to after-dinner speaking

CHARLIE CHESTER

JARROLDS
LONDON

JARROLDS PUBLISHERS (LONDON) LTD
3 Fitzroy Square, London W1

AN IMPRINT OF THE HUTCHINSON GROUP

London Melbourne Sydney Auckland
Wellington Johannesburg Cape Town
and agencies throughout the world

First published 1972

© Charlie Chester 1972

*This book has been set in Baskerville type, printed in Great Britain
on antique wove paper by Anchor Press, and
bound by Wm. Brendon, both of Tiptree, Essex*

ISBN 0 09 110840 3

Contents

Foreword

The thought of making an after-dinner speech to some people is, to say the least, a nightmare, but it need not be so.

Indeed it can be an extreme pleasure, and in the following pages I will endeavour to help you to make your speech the best thing of the evening.

There are stories, one-liners and jokes in abundance to suit all occasions, together with a psychological approach in the preparation of your speech.

Whichever way you look at it, or listen to it, after-dinner speaking is an entertainment and any raconteur worth listening to is something of a humorist chef. The speech is a meal and the balanced ingredients, carefully assembled and served up correctly, can satisfy and tickle the palate, just as much as the food it follows.

To know that you have a good speech in hand is a source of confidence. It is essential, therefore, to spend a little time on it. I trust that you will find this book a help in compiling your speech so that you too can enjoy the meal, and when you rise you will do so with a command of your own and when you next sit down, know that you have 'done a good one' and hear the applause that you have justly earned.

I

How to Prepare Your Speech

In the first place, what are the 'fears' in making a speech? They are probably as follows:
1. How do I start?
2. What the devil can I say?
3. Will they listen to me?
4. Will I make a fool of myself and stumble?
5. What if a previous speaker cracks my best joke?
6. How do I handle a heckler?
7. How do I finish?

In the first instance what you have to say is governed by the Toast which you will be making, or to which you will be replying. It might be a Toast to the Bride and Groom, in which case your task is fairly simple, for it is usually a happy occasion, when the main function is merely to wish the couple well.

Your audience here is conditioned to laugh at almost anything and a little private knowledge about the bridal pair, interlaced with a couple of wisecracks, will suffice. Remember that any young married couple will have their heads and hearts looking to the future and it is therefore advisable to talk in this vein, rather than ruminate on the past. Your ending is obvious and cannot fail because you are asking all concerned to raise their glasses and toast the health of the Bride and Groom. To keep this light it is as well to search for a 'twist' to the proverbial 'we wish them every happiness', such as:

'. . . and in wishing all the best to the Bride and Groom I can only say that I hope they will both be as happy . . . AS MY WIFE AND I THOUGHT WE WERE GOING TO BE!'

Other Toasts might well be:

'The Company' or 'Firm'

'The Society'

'The Press'

'The Past Presidents'

'The Ladies'

'The Guests'

With the task of having to 'propose the Toast', at least you know your function and can prepare it accordingly. Replying to the Toast is a little different, for here you will have heard the Toast and can make a few pencil notes on what the previous speaker has said. You will find that a good rejoinder to a previous remark will score more heavily than a set gag or joke, for repartee is the true wit and ad libbing is always enjoyed, even rehearsed ad libs, for these can be prepared, as I will endeavour a little later to show.

You will probably discover that 'bouncing off' the previous speaker will only enhance the nap hand that you already hold.

Beware of the traps. So many speakers fall into them and one of the deadliest is:

Monotone. There is nothing so dreary as to listen to a man or woman speak in the same level monotone, even if they have something worth listening to; the drone will lull them off to sleep and the interest wanes all too quickly.

Remember to light and shade the voice, up one minute, down the next. Louder at times and then quieter, a little fire here and there and even if you're telling a lie . . . BELIEVE . . . what you are saying. Convince yourself that it's the unvarnished truth, for if *you* don't believe it, you cannot expect others to.

Think back on some of the great orators, like Sir Winston Churchill. You will remember perhaps how he would say everything with conviction:

'NEVER . . . in the field of human conflict . . . have so many owed so much to so few.'

He would growl the emphasis on the correct word and condense a long sentence into the words that would enable him to deliver it in this particular way. He could have said, 'We as a Nation, owe a great debt of gratitude to these fearless airmen, who, though small in numbers have kept the German Air Force at bay, in this our fight for existence,' but he didn't. He chose his words carefully, he used them sparingly and above all he said them with devastating effect.

'We shall fight on the beaches, we shall fight on the landing stages; we shall NEVER surrender.'

As he spoke these words you could almost envisage him with his sleeves rolled up, ready to take on all comers. He said everything with conviction. He would raise and lower his voice; he would make a grand arm gesture and then return his hand to his stomach. Some things he would say threateningly, others with derision and although it would all appear to flow from him as original thought, you can rest assured that it was all well rehearsed.

Although it is important to capture your audience from the start, it is also important that you do not hurry, and whatever you do, make sure that they hear you well—every word. If you make a mistake, make it boldly. Try to remember that you are amongst friends; you have been asked to say a few words and therefore you are acceding to a request.

To show any sign of nerves will undermine your audience more than yourself yet you will find that once you have got them laughing, or even quietly interested, you will settle down and gather confidence as you go along.

A Punch Opening. This is an important factor in the making of a good speech, for if you can 'sock them hard' and make them look up in anticipation you will have won the first round.

To achieve this there are several ways, but one of the safest is to say exactly what they least expect you to say. They anticipate you will say that it is a privilege or a pleasure, so take the opposite view and you will probably get a quick reaction.

Immediately you rise they are going to look at you; so return the gaze, have a good long look at them from end to end of the room. Embrace them all with your gaze so that not one feels left out, for some of the unfortunates will have the worst seats nearest the door and while you are doing this wait for silence. Let them realise that you don't intend to speak until you have their attention.

As you look at them smile and let them see that you have no qualms about speaking, even if your heart *is* pounding like a sledge-hammer. Let your smile tell them that you have every confidence and that indeed you have a few surprises in store . . . not too long, just enough to whet their appetite, then the punch opening.

If, for instance, it's a 'Stag Affair', you might start:

'Gentlemen . . . and I use that word as a CON-VENIENCE!'

I have already indicated that they expect you to say what a pleasure it is—so don't. Spring a surprise and try it another way, something to this effect:

'Ladies and Gentlemen, don't think that this hasn't been a pleasure for me . . . because it HASN'T!'

It is always a good thing to 'knock' yourself or the surroundings. If, for instance, it is a very salubrious place, you might say something like:

'What a beautiful place this is . . . reminds me of home . . . I WAS BORN IN A SLUM!'

It's a strange thing, but the mild insult in a speech is always a sure-fire winner, providing it is done with tongue-in-cheek.

Naturally, if you are designated to speak for a Society or to Toast the Guests, you will have certain information which will be the basis of your talk. All that is required here is to spice it with a few anecdotes. I would advise, however, against the usual, 'it reminds me of a story . . .' preface to a joke. It is so much easier to 'place your joke' in such a way that it blends in with what you are saying.

Instead of saying, 'Did you hear about the man who did so and so . . .' you could append it to someone in your audience, perhaps the previous speaker. This makes the joke more 'live', more believable, and you don't have to announce it as a joke. For as soon as you say, 'Did you hear the one about . . .' you have primed them to expect something; they are looking for the build-up and the tag line. They know it is an untruth and you have lost the element of surprise.

If it is at all possible to know or discover various traits of members of the company, this can be most useful. For instance, if Bill Jones is a well-known lady-killer, you might make a reference to him with the remark that:

'Oh Bill, bless him, he would have been a sex maniac but he couldn't make the medical!'

This is much more sudden and therefore more pungent than saying, 'Did you hear about the fellow . . . who would have been a sex maniac etc. . . .'

Supposing someone was rather fat. You might say what a grand chap he was, ending with:

'. . . of course, I knew him when he only had one stomach!'

You might even refer to him as 'Girth', son of 'Garth'.

If a man is known as a heavy drinker, you might refer to this with something they least expect, and say:

'. . . poor old Joe, he was arrested last week for being sober!'

Here is an example of the opposite view. They expected you to say 'drunk', so you said what they least expected you to say. Another example would be:

'. . . poor old Joe, he got lost in his car last week, didn't know where he was. He rang up the A.A. ALCOHOLICS ANONYMOUS . . . they couldn't help him . . . THEY WERE ALL DRUNK!'

In this effort to punch them from the word go, another little trick is to focus the attention on someone who is very popular and in doing this you reflect that person's popularity and in making him or her laugh, you please the others. An example of this would be the President or Chairman. Obviously they are popular, or they would not be in that exalted position, so you say something nice about the worthy President and throw in a line like:

'. . . look at him, bless him, sitting there smiling . . . AS IF HE WERE IN HIS RIGHT MIND!'

Or something like:

'. . . he's just been voted the man most likely to succeed . . . WHERE A BRUSH WON'T REACH!'

Having then decided on a punch opening and having made sure that you are close enough to the microphone to be heard by everyone in the hall, you then proceed to weave your laughs into what you really have to say. You make sure that you do not maintain a dreary monotone, and you make your speech as entertaining, yet as precise and neat, as you can; for there is nothing worse than 'making weight' by talking and saying nothing. Remember that a speech is ended when it ceases to become either informative or entertaining.

Among the variations of opening gambits a good one is to say that you are deputising for somebody and to give an example. One I recently used was:

'. . . I am deputising tonight for Enoch Powell. He couldn't be here . . . HE'S WITH THE BLACK AND WHITE MINSTRELS!'

Then I followed that up with:

'It's a funny name, Enoch, isn't it? Some people call him eunuch . . . BUT HE ONLY LOST HIS HEAD!'

At the time when the Rolling Stones were first hitting the headlines, remembering their long hair and unkempt appearance gave rise to this opener:

'. . . I'm deputising tonight for the Rolling Stones . . . they are away on a sheep farm . . . BEING DIPPED!'

This was followed up with:

'What about those long hairdos? I understand they are not having their hair cut any more . . . THEY ARE HAVING THEIR EARS LOWER-ED!'

I find it useful to have several little one-liners on any given subject and then use whatever I feel the occasion merits. At the risk of sounding repetitious, I can't emphasise too greatly that the opening gambit *must* command attention, be punchy and say what the audience least expect to hear.

A further example of this is when I spoke at the Press Club to the writers and journalists. I told them:

'Gentlemen, you all have something in common with the great Dr. Johnson . . . HE'S DEAD, TOO!'

If the function had been medical instead of press, I should have used Louis Pasteur, instead of Dr.

Johnson. If it had been a cricket function, I could have substituted W. G. Grace. If it were a jockey, then Fred Archer, and so on. A joke can be used many times by merely changing a name or a word.

For inclusion in an after-dinner entertainment, there is a wide selection of amusing ingredients, but be advised: joke after joke is not the perfect answer. There are:

Anecdotes.

True life incidents . . . and more often than not these are funnier than a concocted story, although most jokes have a basis of truth.

School-boy howlers.

Anagrams.

Boners.

One-liners.

Epigrams.

Monologues.

Shaggy Dog stories and so on.

Without making it too obvious, you take a sprinkling of each and weave them into the overall article, so that you have a variation that is bound to amuse some, if not all, of your listeners.

The triplet word is a good trick and I have used this on several occasions. The triplet word means taking three words that have the same 'ring' to them and which are applied to a particular subject or incident. I can best explain by giving a couple of examples:

When I first went to perform at the Ardwick Hippodrome in Manchester, it struck me that Ardwick was a name which lent itself to comedy and yet those who lived there were obviously so used to it that to them it was just a commonplace name. So I wrote this little four-line verse, as follows:

> I knew a little girl named Ardwick,
> By a cricket ball got struck.
> There's three words on her tombstone now,
> Ardwick . . . 'ard ball . . . 'ard luck.

and there's the triplet.

I rang the changes on this trick when I spoke at the World Sporting Club, which is run by Mr. Boxing himself, Mr. Jack Solomons. I discovered that Jack Solomons was in his early days in the fish business (incidentally a well-known fact). He also owns 29 betting shops. I therefore put the three together as follows: 'And in Jack Solomons's climb to world fame, he has been in the fish business, he has acquired betting shops, and, of course, he represents the world of boxing. And there you have it—CODS . . . ODDS . . . AND SODS!'

There it is again: the triplet. I assure you that it got a howl.

Of course, some jokes in print do not seem quite so funny and everything depends upon the telling. The most important thing here is timing. Begin your build-up with the minimum number of words possible. Paint as graphic a picture as you can, taking the minimum amount of time and then kill it off as suddenly with a tag line.

Another good system is to include the double. This is a joke with an additional ending and if possible a third tag line. Here is an example:

'. . . after all, it's a strange world we're living in. I was reading only last week about the laundry man who knocked on the door of a monastery and asked the head monk if he'd got any . . . DIRTY HABITS!' (laugh) (then the second tag) . . . 'He said NUN!' (laugh) (then the third tag) . . . 'and then he hit him with a PASSING NOVICE!'

Here then is the triple tag line. I wonder if you noticed in the first part that I chose my words carefully and in particular the phrase 'head monk'. His correct title is, of course, the Abbot. However, this spoils the effect of the tag line, which has the same ring to it. The word Abbot, followed by the word Habit, is wrong. Try saying it yourself . . .

'He asked the Abbot if he'd got any dirty habits.'

Perfect English and yet wrong for the raconteur. The word 'monk' brings far more to the imagination and is synonymous with the word 'Habit' which make for perfect reproduction in a tag line. Again, try it yourself . . .

'He asked the head monk if he'd got any dirty habits.'

You may think this is trifling but I assure you that one word can make all the difference to the delivery of a line, especially of a tag line.

It is because of this that I would suggest that you get to know the story or stories of your choice and then narrate them in YOUR OWN way. Phraseology goes hand-in-hand with a person's personality and you will doubtless find that you can deliver the joke far better by talking naturally than by quoting a gag as it is written, or by copying someone else's style.

Depending, of course, upon the function and the type of material the audience is anticipating, it is often possible to make a weak joke strong by the simple use of the word 'bloody' but I would not recommend too frequent use of this.

Some people are extremely good at certain dialects but unless you *are* good at this DON'T try to tell a dialect joke. If, for example, you were in the company of a great number of Jewish people, they would be far more appreciative if you learned an actual Yiddisher phrase and inserted it than if you tried to do a bad Jewish accent.

This applies to other dialects. My advice here is to tell the story your own way rather than spoil it by attempting a bad dialect. If, on the other hand, you are good at dialects, then you have little to worry about, for a whole range of stories lie before you for the taking.

I would again emphasise here that it is far better to refer to living people than say: 'the one about the fellow . . .'

What if the previous speaker cracks your best joke?

You have a choice here. You can either forget it and have something to take its place, or you can make a playful reference to it, such as:

'. . . so-and-so stole my best joke. I wouldn't have minded if he'd cracked it properly . . . but he . . .' (and here you do a gag about the person who told the joke).

If the joke in question was the best thing of the evening you are now sharing in the success of that joke, even though you didn't crack it.

My advice, however, is to forget it, unless it is

important to you. There are plenty of other jokes and you don't want to sound as though you were depending on that particular one to get by.

A theme gimmick.

This is a method which, properly handled, will enhance any speech. It is a system whereby one keeps referring back to the original toast.

Imagine, for example, that you are toasting the Press. You make your opening gambit to the 'Gentlemen of the Press' then each time you arrive at some derogatory remark, probably the tag line of a joke, you say . . . 'which brings me back to the Press'.

Example:

'. . . and the price of things today, it's dreadful, only yesterday I put the down payment on a pork chop . . . even at Victoria Station they've raised the price of the Super Loo to a shilling. THINK OF IT . . . A SHILLING TO GO TO THE TOILET! . . . which brings me back to the Press. We are constantly reminded of the vigil they keep on world events and it only costs us sixpence to buy a copy and realise that the world is full of bloody lunatics . . . which brings me back to the Press.'

This is only a simple example of the repetition and I hope it serves to show you just what I mean by the 'theme gimmick'. It is easy to find a 'theme gimmick' and there are so many variations.

Ad libbing needs a nimble mind which, either through second nature or careful training, can immediately formulate first thoughts into the proper jacket for spontaneous delivery. However, even the most brilliant ad libber will admit that everything he says is not particularly funny, nor witty.

The longer the pause before the ad lib, the lesser the value of the gag and yet, to the professional, it is a mental race against time to quote the immediate thought, without giving offence. If a great number of comedians had actually quoted their first thoughts, without consideration, when ad libbing a particularly offensive heckler, I'm sure many a theatre would have been closed!

Again, when ad libbing, you are passing a remark to 'top' somebody. This is repartee ad libbing. Ordinary ad libbing is speaking 'off the cuff' and this is where a good memory comes in handy for one-liners and quickies.

For instance, if the audience is tough you stop and say:

'How can you sleep with the lights on?'

or,

'I know you are out there; I can hear you breathing.'

Again, if you get an unexpected laugh:

'How can you look so clean and laugh so dirty?'

It is useful to train the mind to automatically think of opposites, for in comedy of all kinds the opposites come into play. It is amazing how the world and everything in it is compiled of opposites—black and white, night and day, man and wife, fish and chips, ham and eggs . . . and you will notice how we have now run into not only opposites but 'natural doubles'; things that automatically go together.

Bearing all this in mind, telling a joke—and indeed just talking—is merely a permutation of words and anything you say can be said many different ways. Fortunately for us words are formulated in such a way that they can mean different things. Take for example this simple sentence:

'Look at those little lambs in that field; they're gambolling.' (This sounds like the word gambling.) The retort might easily be:

'Ah yes, but the older sheep don't, they've been fleeced.'

So there you are, talking about sheep, with an innuendo about something entirely different.

A weaker version of this is what is called 'punning', where you use a word in the wrong context. Most people wince at a pun such as:

'Cigarette world', if you don't smoke. (It's a great world, if you don't smoke.)

This is a particularly bad 'pun' but then I would advise practising punning on any and every subject, no matter how bad the puns. Start handing out the PUNishment! How's this for a start?—an imaginary conversation between a waitress and a customer:

Waitress	HAWAII mister? You must be HUNGARY!
Gent	Yes SIAM, and I can't RUMANIA much longer . . . VENICE lunch ready?
W . . .	I'll RUSSIA table, what'll you HAVRE?
G . . .	Whatever the cook's got ready, but can't JAMAICA step on the gas?
W . . .	ODESSA laugh . . . but ALASKA!
G . . .	Thanks, and put a CUBA sugar in my JAVA!
W . . .	Don't you be SICILY . . . SWEDEN it yourself, I'm only here to SERBIA.

G . . .   DENMARK my cheque, and call the
                 BOSPHOROUS . . . I don't BOLI-
                 VIA know who I am!

W . . .   I don't CARIBBEAN . . . You sure
                 ARARAT!

G . . .   SAMOA your cheek eh? What's got
                 INDIA? Do you think that arguing
                 ALPS business? In any case I think
                 you are rather NICE.

W . . .   Don't KIEV me that BOULOGNE
                 . . . ALAMEIN do! SPAIN in the
                 neck. Pay your cheque and RYDE
                 brother . . . ABYSSINIA!

As you progress your mind will become attuned to
finding the opposites and when somebody makes a
remark you will race to find a 'comeback' that will
'top' whatever has been said. In time you will be
able to hold your own in repartee with most people.

Another good point to remember is the overstatement and understatement, such as:

'She's got so many double chins the bottom one's
going steady with her knee cap.'

This is an overstatement that to some people will
be funny, and the understatement would be something like:

'I wouldn't say she was thin . . . but she's the
only girl I know who can wear a polo-necked sweater
off the shoulders.'

This progresses even further to the distorted joke,
where everything is ludicrously out of proportion,
such as:

'She was so ugly she's the only girl I know who
could use her lower lip for a bathing cap.'

It is a source of amazement how many people will accept an impossible situation in 'joke form'. For example:

'Do you like the suit? I had it made in three days. If it looks a bit lumpy at the back it's the tailor; he's still working on it.'

So there we are. To be an ad libber one must have a command of words, the courage to express the first thought, the ability to find the opposites and to put into words the mental twist.

Supposing for example a man had a particularly short haircut and was preening himself in company. You might feed his ego by saying, 'That's a nice haircut,' and then prick it by saying, 'Did you have it cut from the inside?'

It is, however, the professional raconteur or comedian whose function is to think out new material and ideas, and to the layman it is sufficient to have a small stock of rehearsed ad libs up his sleeve and drop them in when the opportunity arises. You will be amazed how neatly they can fit into the average conversation.

The heckler. When you have the floor, never let a heckler get the better of you. You must use him to your own advantage and it may well be that he can turn out to be a godsend.

The first thing to do if someone shouts something at you is to ask him to repeat it.

'. . . what was that, sir?'

Here, the politeness of the word 'sir' puts you in the 'gentleman' bracket. You are not the aggressor yet! Even if you heard what he said, you ask him to repeat it and this gives you time to think of an answer. You have a choice here of using your own initiative or using a standby.

For instance, supposing a man was drunk and he kept mumbling aloud. You might stop suddenly, focus the attention on him and say:

'. . . pardon me, sir, I'm not interrupting YOU, am I?'

If, for instance, the drunken man shouts something, go along with him until you get the opportunity to top his remarks with something like:

'. . . look, why don't you lean up against the wall? . . . THAT'S PLASTERED AS WELL!'

If someone continues to interrupt you, or mumble aloud, you can usually bring him down to size by a remark like:

'You're very cute—what did you get for Christmas—BLOOD?'
or,

'. . . would you mind keeping that CHILD quiet!'

If they persist, you come down more heavily with, perhaps:

'. . . would you mind standing up, sir? . . . we'd just like to see if the rest of you is as BIG AS YOUR MOUTH!'

This, of course, is only in the extreme. In the main you will find that any heckling at a convivial function is of a light-hearted nature.

How do I finish? This is fairly obvious. If you have made an amusing speech, then do the complete opposite and find a sincere and straight finish. On the other hand, if you have done a fairly straight speech, find a funny ending and sit down on the laugh.

Having now covered the main queries with which I started, let us now recap on the fundamentals:

1. Rise with confidence and let them know by your manner of approach that you have no qualms.
2. Take your time.
3. Make sure you are heard by everyone.
4. Light and shade your voice. Include any mannerisms you find helpful.
5. A punch opening.
6. Be concise. Don't ramble on, groping for words, or mumble.
7. If there was a previous speaker—use him. Make use of his popularity.
8. If you have a heckler, use him as a stooge.
9. Straight or comedy finish according to the rest of your speech.

So much then for the preparation of your speech. Like a chef, you prepare the ingredients and add them to taste. Like the tailor, you have the material; you cut to shape the various panels and stitch them together, and according to the care and attention you put into the work you can expect the reaction you deserve.

There is just one thing here, however: the tailor and the chef are a little different, for one is shaping a garment to fit a particular person while the other is catering for an expected taste. If you order roast lamb, at least you know what it's going to taste like (or at least what it should taste like), but the raconteur, has to address himself to an assortment of mental levels. He can't stop to ask each individual what kind of joke he would like to hear. One assumes that he will accept what you give him, and the best way to do this is to select your material and base it on the accepted level of the mentality of the assembled company.

It has been known that some speakers feel almost a hostility before they begin, but a good speaker can surmount this by his delivery and choice of words. Let's face it—there's nothing better than a good challenge! Indeed one might say that it is a bigger feather in one's cap to win someone over, than to aim jokes at someone who would laugh at anything.

Nevertheless, I would like you to feel that you can toy with your audience knowing that you have the power to make them follow your every word.

The Mechanics and Psychology of Humour

For the benefit of those who may be interested in the higher 'mechanics' of humour let us now perform an autopsy on the subject. What is funny? Why do people laugh? Indeed, why should something be funny to someone and yet unfunny to another?

These are questions that must be asked and where possible the answer found. After all, to be a good doctor one must be able to diagnose as well as prescribe. It would naturally follow that the better the diagnosis, the more direct the prescription and the quicker the treatment.

Let us then take humour to pieces and see what makes it tick.

In the first place, there can be no such thing as a 'sense' of humour. There is no 'SENSE' of humour, it is an emotion; and of all the human emotions HUMOUR IS THE MOST FICKLE.

You do not have to be reminded that you love your wife, mother, or sweetheart. The emotion of love is so deeply embedded that it rises to the surface at the slightest call.

The same thing can be said of hate, pity, sympathy
—they are all strongly rooted in us—and yet . . .
you DO have to be reminded of a joke that made
you laugh. In fact, I doubt if anyone could truly
say which day he laughed the most and recall the
incident or joke which made him laugh.

How many times have you heard someone say,
'I heard a good one the other day . . . I WISH I
COULD REMEMBER IT.'?

If someone makes an unkind remark to you, you
remember it for a long time because it hurt you, but
if someone amuses you, you laugh and then promptly
forget it. Such is the fickleness of humour.

This may well be because humour is only a hair-
line away from pathos, and in any case cruelty is
one of the main ingredients that make us laugh.

The natural progression for a joke is:

    IMAGINATION
    ANTICIPATION
    CULMINATION
    CRUELTY

Yes, basically we *are* cruel, but it's not our fault;
we were born that way. As children we laughed at
Punch and Judy and there was never a more cruel
pair, for they constantly whacked each other with
clubs, and I can remember them, hanging each
other from gallows.

We have always laughed at the clown who was
constantly falling down.

The mishaps of the Keystone Cops made us shout
with laughter, and who did not revel in CHARLIE
CHAPLIN'S misfortunes?

The axiom for every principal comic in pantomime

was PLAY FOR SYMPATHY. Buttons in Cinderella
. . . he never got the girl and we were sorry for
him.

Sympathy and affection then are the closest
emotions to humour on one side, and cruelty is the
closest on the other.

Let us now, in a simple experiment, go through
the four ingredients as I listed them.

Imagination. This is one of the most vivid and
flexible workings of the human mind. It is therefore
the principal ingredient of the comic to work on.

IMAGINE a fat man walking down the street . . .
Once I have said that, your imagination takes over,
the seed is set.

Then I say, 'NO, forget that,' . . . but you won't,
it's too late, your imagination is already at work.

I then say, 'There's a banana skin lying on the
pavement.' NOW you put the two together and the
second stage takes over.

Anticipation. You start to anticipate what you
THINK is going to happen between the fat man
and the banana skin. Like a child who gets more
pleasure in unwrapping the parcel than in the actual
present, you are getting pleasure in what you THINK
will happen.

Then comes stage three. CULMINATION.

You knew it! He stepped on to the banana skin
and up he went—BANG!

You are very self-satisfied because you knew it
was going to happen. . . . You were clever; you
guessed—and in any case it wasn't *you* who banged
the back of your head.

And there is the final stage. CRUELTY.

The fat man bumped his head. It was undignified, not to mention painful, and you laughed. . . .

So much for the simple progression—imagination, anticipation, culmination and cruelty . . . but WAIT!

Suddenly you see blood coming from that man's ear.

The smile is wiped off your face and you think, my God, he really *has* hurt himself . . . badly.

What was funny a moment ago is no longer funny. The emotion of pity or sympathy has now taken over . . . it has completely swamped the sense of humour.

All it took to switch you from what was funny to what was unfunny was the split second it took to see blood.

I hope that this simple example serves to show just how fickle Dame Humour can be.

What do we laugh at?

There are several things that make us laugh. Self-satisfaction is one. It's something like the feeling of security a child experiences when tucked up in a nice warm bed while the wind and snow are doing their worst outside.

Whether we like to admit it or not, we are all pretty fond of ourselves. We like to think that we are either 'presentable' in appearance, or clever, or much-travelled and we try to suppress this self-satisfaction behind a mask of modesty. . . . But it is there and without it we would not be human.

Security is another thing that allows us to laugh.

When someone makes a joking reference to an old tramp, our imagination begins to work with the secure knowledge that the tramp is so far removed from us . . . he could never *be* us, and this 'security' of mind comes to the fore in the human phenomena of humour.

The distortion of truth is the basis for a joke or a comedy situation.

Close proximity to truth and self is another. Something that reflects ourselves makes us laugh.

The tearing-down of elegance and the unseating of pomposity are other things that make us laugh because these are another form of SECURITY and CRUELTY.

Let us take a simple instance.

Supposing you were a schoolboy and as you ran across the playground your trousers fell down. It would not be very funny. BUT IF IT HAPPENED TO YOUR PLAYMATE you would probably laugh.

The security in the fact that it did not happen to you enables you to laugh at another's discomfort. NOW LET US TAKE THIS A STEP FURTHER. Let us add elegance to the same situation. Imagine that instead of a schoolboy running across a playground, a princess is elegantly walking across the lawns at Buckingham Palace. Suddenly, amid all the pomp, her knickers fall down! Wow!

Either you are shocked and filled with sympathy for her embarrassment, or it will be funnier than the schoolboy's trousers. We have destroyed elegance, and therefore added spice to the situation.

In the same way, word comedy is a line from A to B distorted. If you take a simple sentence like: 'That

B

girl has got a lovely head of hair.' It is a straight line and there is nothing wrong with it, then you distort it by saying:

'. . . trouble is, it's all on her chin!'

You have now bent the end of the straight line and have made a mental picture which is distorted, and someone laughs.

In professional circles this is called the 'tag line' or the 'pay-off'. It would be wrong to bend the line in the middle, for no one expects to laugh in the middle of a joke which then continues, only to fizzle out. This would be an anti-climax, so it naturally follows that the twist always comes at the end.

Notwithstanding what I have just said, there are certain occasions and certain jokes which are so devised that one, two and even three tag lines are used. This is what is known as patter. Let us take a subject, say a man on a bus; the raconteur says something like:

'I saw this fellow on the bus with a shocking great boil on his neck. I wouldn't say it was big, but the conductor charged him half fare for it! [Here is the first laugh.] I said to him, "It wasn't very nice of the conductor to charge you half fare for that." He said, "I didn't mind; the last one made me poke it under the stairs!" [The second laugh.] I said, "Well, why don't you get something for it?" He replied, "I have, I've just bought a haversack!" ' (The third laugh.)

Note here that if it made you smile at all, this was due to your innate sense of cruelty, plus the fact that many of us have suffered from a boil. Here we have the close proximity of truth. A reflection of ourselves.

There are two types of comedy. Sight and sound.

Of these, sight comedy is the first comedy and to explain this in a simple way let us take for example a tiny baby in a cot.

If you leaned over and whispered, 'kitchy koo', with a dead pan face, I doubt if you would get any registered result.

BUT . . . and here you might notice that most mothers are born with the psychology, IF you pull a funny face and say, 'kitchy koo', it is odds on that you might evoke a toothless grin.

The baby realises by the funny face and tone of voice that you are being funny . . . the sound then permeates, and it is the VISUAL that makes the child ready to receive the funny sound.

How many times have you witnessed someone nod to a tiny baby and say something like . . . 'who is a bootiful ittel man then, eh?'? The child smiles. It obviously doesn't know what is being said, but it knows by the pleasant face, the nodding of the head and lastly by the tone of voice, that someone is trying to amuse it.

Sight comedy then is the first to register, simply because it is immediate. One doesn't have to 'work it out'.

Verbal comedy is more intricate, for words can mean many things, and what is funny to some will by very unfunny to others.

Incongruity and distortion are prime factors, and easily done with words. There have even been distortions of distortions. Recently there have been a spate of 'sick' jokes.

'Mummy, why do I keep running round in circles?'

'Be quiet, or I'll nail your other foot to the floor!'

Even words themselves have been distorted. Remember Lewis Carroll!

'. . . the slithy toves did gyre and gimble in the wabe.'

Stanley Unwin, the master of 'double talk', made a great impact upon the public and he is able to do with consumate ease what most of us find very difficult; that is to distort words as he goes along. He might greet you with something like:

'Greetings . . . deep joy . . . grabbit the warmer and shakey. Joy to the eyebolds, meeting you like this in the early maud, is enough to warm the cocklode of the heartsprings . . .'

It sounds right . . . and yet it sounds wrong . . . it is nearly truth and has been distorted. The sincerity with which it is delivered makes us laugh.

Telling a joke is like digging a pit . . . the audience either falls into it, or jumps over it. The art of telling a joke is only to tell what is necessary, so that the listener cannot race you to the tag line.

What happens when we laugh? The answer might amaze some people, for when we laugh heartily for a prolonged session, we take a great deal out of ourselves.

You must have heard the expression 'helpless with laughter', or 'my sides ached'. Of course they did; the speaker has made you use muscles that haven't been used for a long time.

This is what actually happens when we laugh at a joke.

Firstly, we listen, and our ears are working. Next the brain takes over and our imagination is titillated.

We then separate the incongruous from the normal, which in turn starts a whole process of reactions in the human form.

Our face muscles begin to work. We smile.

We open our throats to take deep breaths and emit pleasurable sounds (laughter).

The throat muscles are at work.

The larynx rattles away.

We throw our heads back as we rock.

Then the tear glands start to work and we cry with laughter.

We rock our bodies backwards and forwards and if you want proof of this stand sideways to an audience when they are laughing. They look like a field of corn in a high wind.

Next the thorax (lungs), ribs, etc., are working hard.

The abdomen (the stomach) goes in and out.

We bang our knees.

We stamp our feet.

So there we are . . . from top to toe we are convulsed and working so hard that a laughter session can tire us . . . and NO WONDER.

The body uses so much adrenalin that we beg . . . 'Please, no more . . . don't make me laugh any more.'

Simple humour is that which needs no analysing, such as little four-line jingles . . . and we began our education with these when we were children.

Little Jack Horner sat in the corner,
Eating his Christmas pie,
He put in his thumb and pulled out a plum,
And said, 'What a good boy am I.'

Later in life we bring imagination to it more deeply and we still enjoy jingle, but with a little auto-suggestion.

> There was a young lady named Hopper,
> Who came a society cropper,
> She went to Ostend, with a gentleman friend,
> And the rest of the story's improper.

Now you start to draw your own conclusions on what was improper, and you smile.

Then there are the types of jingle that are based on word-play such as:

> A fly and a flea in a flue,
> Were imprisoned, so what could they do?
> Said the fly, 'Let us flee'
> 'Let us fly,' said the flea.
> And they flew through a flaw in the flue.

It is strange how intelligent people will accept the impossible fact of animals talking. This is known as the Shaggy Dog story.

Two camels were walking along in the desert and one said to the other, 'I don't care what they say . . . I'M THIRSTY!'

Then there is the build-up to the let-down. This is where there is no joke at all, and for an example:

Two hippopotamuses (or is it hippopotami?) were lying in the sun by the river bank, sunning themselves. Suddenly one turned to the other and said, 'Agnes, I don't know why, but I keep thinking today is Wednesday.'

It is the incongruity of the remark that makes you smile, not the fact that two hippos were talking. You have accepted that.

Other great assets to the raconteur are two factors.

Exaggeration and minimising.

These are carried to a considerable degree, thereby creating a deviation from the truth and finally to distortion, such as:

'I ran my fingers through her wavy hair . . . then I realised her hair was straight . . . it was her head that was wavy!'

'She wore a little black velvet band round her neck. I asked her why she wore it . . . she took it off to show me, and her head fell off!'

'I kissed her on the back of the neck . . . that's where her lips were!'

'She had lips like velvet . . . I kissed them and got a mouthful of moths!'

and so on.

You will notice too that alluding to one thing and referring to another will assist in the formation of a funny remark.

Take, for example, a man with a big nose . . . there is nothing particularly funny about a big nose, but to refer to something else and combine the two might result in a remark like:

'Excuse me, is that your nose, or are you eating a banana?'

Then there is THE ETERNAL TWIST.

No matter what subject you pick on, there are always several ways of making jokes about it.

Take the simple subject of big feet. In the case of

repartee (two people talking) it might register like
this:

'Get off my foot!'

'Sure, is it much of a walk?'

In the single idiom it might be:

'Big feet! She didn't wear boots . . . canal barges
with laceholes'

or,

'For shoes she wore orange crates, half-soled.'

So you see, every subject is full of twists and
permutations.

Now we return to emotions. These have to be
watched very carefully by the comic, for emotion
can mar someone's enjoyment of what was meant
to be a joke.

If there were one hundred men in a room and one
was in love with, or married to, a bow-legged girl,
and a joke was told, it may well be that ninety-nine
men would laugh.

Supposing the joke-teller said:

'That dancer . . . she was so bow-legged, when she
pirouetted across the stage . . . she looked like an egg
beater!'

The man in love with a bow-legged girl would
probably think that very unfunny. The emotion of
love would not allow the emotion of humour to
come to the fore.

This then has to be watched, for people tend to
become emotionally involved in many things:
Work. Religion. Politics. Personal afflictions such
as bald heads, stuttering, cross eyes and so on.

It is easy to make jokes on all these things but they
are funny only to those who do not suffer from them.

Political jokes are not appreciated by fanatics of one sect or another, but are usually safe ground, for we return here to the undermining of officialdom and knocking pomposity.

To take the mickey out of a workman is mildly funny, to take it out of the foreman is funnier, to take it out of the director is funnier still.

Another important factor in the telling of a joke is to draw the picture verbally and define it as sharply as you can. If you made a joke based on a fat lady and a thin man, it would be better to allude to an actual well-proportioned lady, an acknowledged fat person, for this will draw the picture more accurately.

For our fat lady joke we must find an actual place: to say she was walking down the street is rather negative . . . neither here nor there. Let us, therefore, place the person and the venue.

So we have: Tessie O'Shea was walking down Bond Street. The picture is now alive . . . our imagination can visualise the actual person without even stating that she is a fat lady. We can see Bond Street. It is all believable . . . and so we go on.

Tessie O'Shea was walking down Bond Street and she bumped into Cardew Robinson (or any other well-known thin man). She said, 'Hello, Cardew, you look as though there's been a food shortage!' And Cardew said, 'Yes, and you look as though you CAUSED it!'

And there we are—a joke based on a fat lady and a thin man which has the semblance of truth. They have been chosen from real life and it is easy to imagine that this actually happened.

Now we come to the family tree.

Getting down to rock-bottom there are only twelve main 'institutions' from which spring this entire world with its families of jokes.

They are as follows:

The Human Form	this incorporates	Physical defects Habits Drunkenness Baldness Wigs False teeth, etc.
Marriage	this incorporates	Henpecked husbands Nagging wives The lodger Children Marriage service Bridesmaids Best man, etc.
Trades & Professions	incorporate	Occupations Workmen Courtroom Clergy Doctors Actors Unions, etc.
Sex	this incorporates	Flirting Courting Love Girl friend Breach of promise Personality, etc.
Services	incorporate	Army Navy Air Force Schools Domestic service, etc,

Wiseguy	this incorporates	Repartee Humorous retorts, etc.
Animal Life	this incorporates	Domestic animals Pets Wild animals Circus Farm, etc.
Pastimes	incorporate	Sport Boxing Games Practical jokes Swimming Singing Instrument playing, etc.
Accident	this incorporates	Taxi drivers Motorists Traffic Nurse Hospital Police Insurance, etc.
Food	this incorporates	Chef Restaurant Waiters Waitresses Menu Proprietor Indigestion, etc.
Ghosts	incorporate	Nerves Fright Haunted house, etc.
Nonsense	this incorporates	Silliness Double talk Hokum Jargon, etc.

Well, there they are: twelve institutions from which come our entire library of chuckles. Of course, there are many other subjects, but I have only laid out the general first-thought items that spring from the main sources.

The Shaggy Dog Story, for instance, could be applied either to Animal Life or to Silliness, which I have put under the heading of Nonsense. Those are the twelve 'hardies', from which you can make up or choose any story.

So much then for some of the mechanics of humour. It is the subject in itself for an entire book, but I hope that it will give you food for thought and the realisation that to make someone laugh is a worthwhile pastime with a greater depth than some people would imagine.

If you think sufficiently about the subject, you might be amazed at what you can discover about other people and what they laugh at. It is a fascinating subject and I hope that some of the things I have listed will help you to use the flexibility of words, to watch for conflicting emotions, and to enjoy the fact that you have explored some of the mysteries of what we call our 'sense of humour'.

I now offer you a selection of openers, ad libs, and stories, grouped under headings in alphabetical order for your easy selection, from which I hope you will find something to suit the occasion.

MISCELLANEOUS OPENERS AND ONE LINERS TO CHOOSE FROM

Ladies and gentlemen . . . and looking around I use that term very loosely.

Ladies and gentlemen . . . well, that's the rehearsed bit and from here on it's nerve.

Ladies and gentlemen . . . and having said that the deterioration starts.

Ladies and gentlemen, I'd like to say what a pleasure this is. I'd LIKE to but I just can't.

This being National Sex Week, do remember that if you've given at the office, you don't have to give at home.

Gentlemen, and I'll repeat that word GENTLE-MEN. I did that because it's the best part of my speech. The rest of it is crap, but then so was the dinner.

You've heard of Sinatra the voice—Gable the legs . . . you're looking at THE LUMP.

Thank you. I've never heard so much applause since the day I threatened to leave home.

Thank you for that lovely reception—the sound of handcuffs made me feel at home.

ART

1.   Here's a great name for an Art Gallery . . . Paintings A Gogh-Gogh!
2.   I'm very keen on painting, especially still life. So far I've done 15 railway porters!

3.   You can never make a success of art until you've suffered, and I've suffered. Well, you try holding your crayons, with people walking all over your hands.

4.   She's a strange girl, she's a model for a modern painter. She was sitting there, with three cups of coffee—one for each mouth!

5.   You know if Picasso painted her portrait, it would look like her.

6.   When I was sixteen I went to Art School to paint life studies. When I was seventeen they made me buy a brush.

7.   I've just finished a painting of the wife. Oh it's life-like. No sooner had I put the finishing touches to the mouth than it started asking for money!

BARBER

1.   The barber said to me, 'Would you like your hair singed?' I said, 'Yes.' He said, 'You're dead lucky—the shop's on fire!'

2.   I said to the barber, 'Look, I don't want any mention of the weather, sport or politics.' After five minutes he whispered, 'That's a pity.' I said, 'What do you mean, a pity?' He said, 'Well, it's pouring with rain and your car's outside with the hood open, somebody's pinched your golf bag, and our local M.P. has just left his lighted cigar butt on that chair and you're sitting on it.'

3.   Skinhead to barber . . . 'Gimme a Pan American . . . that's straight over by clipper.'

4.   Long-haired youth sat in the barber's chair and surprised the barber by asking for a haircut. The barber looked at his shoulder-length locks and said, 'Are you sure you want it cut?' the youth said, 'Yes.' Dutifully the barber began work and after working for 5 minutes on it he said, 'Excuse me, didn't you go to Dulwich College?' The surprised youth said, 'Yes, how did you know?' The barber said, 'I've just found your bloody cap!'

BEATNIKS—HIPPIES, ETC

1.   One poor fellow was sitting there suffering from an emotional shock—he'd just had a bath!

2.   Now they've got Beatniks Anonymous—any danger of one of them having a wash, the others belt round and turn the water off.

3.   I've got a Beatnik housekeeper—comes in twice a week to dirty the place up.

4.   The last Beatnik party I was invited to the Airwick went down in the bottle waving a white flag.

5.   I saw one girl leaning up against the bar, black leather jacket, black stockings and boots . . . looked like an umbrella rolled up.

6.   All this long hair makes things difficult. Two of them got married and the vicar said, 'Who's going to take who to be what?'

7.   They get married so young these days—they're thinking of replacing the holy water with gripe-water.

8.   Flower people—they look more like neglected graves.

9.   When the skinheads go to the seaside the tide's too nervous to come in.

10.   With mods, rockers and skinheads having their usual summer jaunts to the coast, the shops are full of novelties . . . bandages, splints, coshes, flick-knives.

BOXING

1.   (of a boxer) For years he's had his nose in the ring . . . looks as if he's had the ring in his nose.

2.   I was respected at school; you see I was a boxer. I remember one fight, I kept saying to myself, 'I'm gonna win, I'm gonna win.' It didn't do any good though, I know what a liar I am.

3.   After the fight I was grinning from ear to ear—no teeth.

4.   My opponent had one of those Sunday punches—when he hit you, you landed on your 'weak end'. I shook him, suddenly I brought one up from the floor—which is where I happened to be at the time. That really made him mad. I didn't know whether to put up my hands and fight like a man, or put up my ears and run like a rabbit.

5.   Suddenly I was cautioned for holding—so I

let go of the referee. Then my opponent threw eight punches at me, I didn't feel one of them—I was out cold when the first one landed. I kept my head, I lost the rest of me but I kept my head.

6.   He had me in the corner so long I had a triangular back.

7.   Then I started bobbing and weaving, bobbing and weaving, weaving and bobbing. I didn't win the fight but I finished three baskets and a Persian rug.

8.   After the fight they gave me a big cup—to keep my teeth in.

CARS AND MOTORING

1.   There's two kinds of pedestrians here—the quick and THE DEAD!

2.   If you see a car going up the street with boots dangling from it you don't know whether it's been a wedding . . . OR AN UNLUCKY PEDESTRIAN!

3.   I'm a bit worried about my car—if I don't trade it in soon I'll own it.

4.   I bought a new car two years ago, haven't driven it yet, it's still in the show-room. Well, where else can you park it?

5.   Everybody drives these days—my girl friend's at it—taking lessons. She went to her instructor yesterday—TOOK HIM SOME GRAPES!

6.   She made a silly mistake, understandable, she lost her nerve driving in a tunnel! Well, who

wouldn't with the GLASGOW EXPRESS COMING AT YOU!

7.   The service in my local garage is marvellous. I pulled in yesterday and before I could say a word they'd lifted my bonnet, filled me with water, cleaned out my sump, wiped the paintwork over and oiled my bearings. I thought that was pretty good—especially as I was on a bike at the time!

8.   Joe's got a smashing car. It's fitted with special monster windscreen wipers . . . it wipes pedestrians off the windscreen!

9.   (So and so) . . . is a shocking driver, he's been invited to play gearbox in the London Philharmonic.

10.   Hasn't passed his test yet . . . he goes out every morning to practise. Last Sunday morning he was out before eight o'clock . . . even then he knocked two people flying and you can't say it was their fault—they were indoors having breakfast at the time!

11.   Anyway, a lot seems to have happened since I was here last, they're getting tougher on the motorists. I was threatened with three years on my way here—and that was for a dirty number plate!

12.   I've got a lovely little car. I'm proud of it. Two more payments and I'll be able to drive it about in the daytime.

13.   Actually it's one of those underslung jobs, if you want to get in the back seat you have to come up through a manhole cover.

14.   Still it was a nice day and in the evening we hired a coach for a mystery drive—you know the type of thing—THEY BLINDFOLD THE DRIVER!

15.   It seems they're constantly introducing new road signs for the benefit of Continentals over in the British Isles. There's one showing a car half-way up a brick wall—that means no through road. There's another sign of a train going over a bridge—that means look out for falling mail bags. If you see a bull's head—reverse quickly; you're in the middle of a field. If you see two cars on top of each other— that means the road narrows suddenly.

16.   It's no fun motoring to the seaside these days, there's so much traffic about. The last time I went I had to get out of the car three times—to make payments on it!

17.   I recently bought a car on actors' terms. 50% down and the rest in 24 hours.

18.   A great big cop came up to me and said, 'Now, about your car . . .' I said, 'You can cut that right out, I haven't been speeding, I've got a driving licence, I've got a road fund licence, I've got a registration book and a certificate of insurance.' He said, 'That may be, but you haven't got a car— it's just been pinched!'

CHRISTMAS

1.   This year it will be I saw Mummy nagging Santa Claus!

2.   At Christmas time they don't hang up stockings in Russia . . . they hang up suspicious relatives!

3.   . . . and that turkey I bought for Christmas,

I wouldn't say it was old, it didn't have drumsticks, it had walking sticks. Some birds have feathers—not this one—it had a long red coat and a row of medals!

4.   Some people can be very hurtful. I remember when I went out carol singing, I stood at one big house and I sang four carols, then I knocked on the door and a tuning fork came through the letter box.

5.   Don't you get some funny things at the Christmas sales? I got a broken arm!

6.   What a Christmas! All the fuss we had over plucking our chicken—you never saw such a mess, feathers all over the place. I wish I'd taken it outside and killed it first!

7.   Last year Santa Claus left me a bundle of I.O.Us.

8.   I had a nice Christmas card from the Ministry of Health and Social Security. It read as follows:

Free wigs and teeth the National Gift,
This Christmas message heed it.
You're three years now behind with stamps.
Good health—you're gonna need it.

9.   Workmanship isn't the same these days. Even the mottoes in the Christmas crackers aren't finished. I pulled one the other day and two script writers fell out.

CLUB, FIRM OR ASSOCIATION

1.   (of a football team manager) He's teaching them speedway riding . . . he figures it's the only way he'll get them to Wembley.

2.   (the following could be applied to any person or team, i.e. managing director or goal keeper) . . . Joe had a good idea for (so and so) . . . but he couldn't get a licence for the GUN.

3.   It was an enormous place and I said to him, 'How many people work here?' He said, 'About half of them.'

4.   I'm told that they hand you out the biggest pay packets in the country here—and before you know it they'll be putting wages in them.

5.   He took me to his office and on the wall was an inscribed tablet in memory of those who had asked for a rise.

6.   They're all so happy working at the factory here—they tell me that when the hooter goes Joe has to be driven home with a whip.

7.   I was talking to the foreman and I said, 'I bet you've got some clever people working here.' He said, 'Not likely, it's the clever ones that don't work.'

8.   The poor girl in the office. Work! . . . inside eight hours she'd knitted herself a twin set.

9.   I asked one girl what she did and she said, 'I'm a pencil sharpener's assistant.' I watched her at work. They stick a pencil on her ear and she does six back somersaults. It doesn't sharpen the pencil but it keeps the boys awake.

10.   The office staff—they're the people who buy midday papers on their way to work.

11.   He said to me, 'The boys here have seen the writing on the wall.' I said, 'Seen it? . . . they put it there.'

12.   I saw two of the directors outside, wiping their feet on the same shop steward.

13.   A foreman—that's a flat tyre in the wheel of progress.

14.   A foreman—that's a bottle neck with skin.

15.   A foreman—a broken cog in the chain of industry.

16.   A shop steward—a man who does dirty work with clean hands.

COUNTRYSIDE

1.   I was reading about a farmer who was milking a cow. The poor thing got struck by lightning and the farmer was left holding the bag!

2.   Mind you this weather makes you realise the beauties of the English countryside, the rolling green, the pastures, the trees, the flowers, the hedgerows . . . it's all there. Buried beneath lemonade bottles, fag packets, cartons, courting couples!

3.   What a summer we've had. I feel sorry for the farmers. One of them planted 200 acres of corn and at harvest time he brought in half a ton of mackerel. Fortunately his potato harvest saved him.

He was the only farmer in the country flogging fish and chips wholesale.

4.   Automation is the new thing now—it's even got to the farms. The animals are catching on, I see a sow has just had a happy event—FOUR TINS OF HAM!

5.   I walked into the farmhouse, there were three shorthorns, two Rhode Island Reds and a Nanny-goat—listening to The Archers!

6.   You can tell it's nearing the mating season—all the hedgehogs are wearing a puzzled look.

7.   Spring is on the way, I heard a hedgehog serenading his sweetheart—he was singing, 'You Always Hurt The One You Love'.

8.   She was telling me about her brother, he's a clever boy, he's got a farm—he's been crossing porcupines with sheep so that they can knit their own jumpers. Mind you, if it's not successful he's not worried. With feet his size he can always get a job stamping out forest fires.

9.   Ah, Spring! I saw a little robin sitting on a holly bush with a tear in its eye—and you'd have a tear in your eye if you were sitting on a holly bush!

10.   The farm was in a shocking state of repair. It was the only farm I know where the duckpond is inside the house.

11.   Just found out why the cow jumped over the moon . . . the fellow who milked her had cold hands.

12.   During the war a young fellow was seen sitting milking a cow, whereupon a high-ranking official frowned at him and said, 'Why aren't you

at the front?' The youth replied, 'Don't be so bloody daft—the milk's this end.'

13. Two rabbits were being chased by a couple of foxes—they both ran up a tree and one said to the other, 'What do we do now?' The other one said, 'Let's stay up here till we outnumber them!'

14. A spinster decided to take up poultry farming so she went to market to purchase a dozen hens and a dozen cockerels. She was advised that she would only need one cockerel. However, she insisted on taking the twelve saying, 'I know what it feels like to be left out.'

CRICKET

1. I remember my first cricket match—as I hit a four for the boundary the crowd rose as one man —come to think of it it was . . . ONE MAN!

2. He looked a picture walking out of the pavilion with his white ducks. He looked disgusting when the white ducks flew away and left him stark naked.

3. An old gentleman and his wife were sitting watching the cricket and after a while the old boy dropped off to sleep. Just then, the bowler bowled . . . the batsman clouted it for six into the crowd. It landed with a thud on the head of the sleeping man . . . He awoke with a start, scowled at his wife and said, 'I know I asked you to give me a nudge but that's bloody ridiculous.'

DOGGEREL

1. Old Mother Hubbard, she went to the
        cupboard,
    To get her Alsatian some bread,
    When she got there, the cupboard was bare,
    So she ate the Alsatian instead.

2. A Farmer's girl called Mary Lawn,
    Was milking a cow with a crumpled horn,
    The cow went mad and kicked poor Mary,
    Once in the cowshed and twice in the dairy.

3. There was a young fellow called Vickers,
    Who met a young girl in the flickers,
    He saw some pink wool and started to pull,
    And he found he'd unravelled her knitting!

4. There was a cow stood in a field,
    The silly cow she wouldn't yield,
    The reason why she wouldn't yield
    She didn't like her udders feeled.

FOOD

1. You should try the new dish they've got, it's called Treble Chance. Three to one it doesn't kill you.

2. I don't know quite what to make of the soup. It's too thick to drink and too thin to plough!

3. I had just got started on a nice meaty bone in my soup when the chap sitting next to me snatched

it away. Mind you, you couldn't blame him; it was his elbow.

4.   . . . but her food's so bad the mice eat out.

5.   We had a peculiar meal, they roll the peas round a circular table and if they land in your lap they're yours!

6.   The dinner was austere—as a matter of fact I saw the horse steered into the kitchen.

7.   Talk about bad manners at the table—I reached out for the hors-d'œuvres—next minute I was part of it.

8.   The food at the digs wasn't too bad. Every day we had a choice of two things—take it or leave it.

9.   And the food . . . it was the same every day, dressed crab six days running. On Sunday they put a clean collar on it.

10.   She cooks the kind of meals that puts colour into your face—purple!

11.   We were sitting down to cold meat as it struck eleven and it surprised me because it's the first time I've ever heard cold meat strike eleven. Mind you, there's been plenty of other meat strikes.

12.   The cook had falling hair—it's the first time I've had cottage pie with a thatched roof. Before I could stick a knife and fork in it the Borough Surveyor walked in and condemned it.

FOOTBALL

1.   Footballers are so well paid these days they're getting worried. I overheard a couple chatting in their dressing room the other day, one of them had got a transfer. He said the home games were the trouble—his wife had been seen three times in the same mink!

2.   What a football match! I was in the crush outside the gates and I called out to one fellow. I said, 'Do you think you'll get in?' He said, 'I hope so, I'm the referee!'

3.   Fellow at a football match was swaying from side to side and this was driving the man behind him mad. After a while the man behind him tapped him on the shoulder and said, 'Cut out the swaying from side to side, mate, I can't see what's going on.' Whereupon the man said, 'I'm sorry, friend, only I was 25 years in the Navy and it's a habit.' The man behind swayed backwards and forwards and said, 'I've got 14 kids but I'm not worrying you, am I?'

GENTLEMEN

1.   (of a singer) Unfortunately he was drowned by the band. Mind you, a brick round the neck would have been CHEAPER.

2.   He's an optimist and you all know what an optimist is . . . it's a man of 70 who marries a girl of 20 and looks for a house near a school.

3.   He got married at 63. Well, he doesn't drink and he doesn't smoke—I suppose that was all there was left! Married at 63, the secret is out now—at the wedding they threw confetti at her and pep pills at him!

4.   He's got such a shaggy moustache, it's like looking at the world through shredded wheat. It looks as if his face was run over by a combine harvester!

5.   He's a real swashbuckler. Mind you, he's beginning to buckle where he used to swash!

6.   He loved women. I don't know what he died of, but it took the undertaker three days to wipe the smile off his face.

7.   A man's as old as he looks and if he only looks he is old.

8.   He had satisfaction written right across his face—and you need a hell of a big face to get a word like that on it.

9.   I would have painted his portrait but I couldn't get enough yellow paint and wrinkled canvas.

10.   He's a smashing runner, well he has to be, he's been taking ballet lessons and the school was right next to the Naval Barracks!

11.   That man's always got his face in the press—I think that's how he got it that shape!

12.   Poor old (so and so) he had a nasty black eye—I think he coughed in a wardrobe!

13.   He had his moment of triumph a few years ago—they used his mouth as a model for the Blackwall Tunnel!

14.   I was going to buy him a present for Christ-

mas, something to keep him warm—but where can you buy blood?

15.   He's a clever man, he's been crossing chickens with parrots and every morning they bang on the back door with a spoon and shout, 'Come and get it.'

16.   If kissing is a certain way of spreading germs he must be the unhealthiest man in town.

17.   I mean, there must be something wrong with a man who can wear a monocle and look through it with both eyes.

18.   Poor fellow, he got the sack from his last place—they caught him taking his coat off.

19.   He is quite a thinker and when I say thinker —I'm lisping.

20.   He's a man that knows what hard work is— that's why he's never done any.

21.   I don't think he's got much of a sense of humour because I said to him one night, 'I think your wife's just fallen out of a third floor window.' He said, 'Don't make me laugh, I've got a sore lip.'

22.   Look at him, what a suit, he told me he got it for a song—must have been ragtime.

23.   I've heard of a crew haircut but that's ridiculous. He's got hardly any crew left—and they're standing by to abandon ship. I don't suppose you can blame them—empty vessels!

24.   There are no flies on that lad—well, even flies can be fussy.

25.   There are no flies on that lad—but if you look closely you can see where they've been!

26.   He's saving up for his old age. Next week he starts spending it!

27.   When I first met him he was singing, 'My Love Is Like a Red Red Rose.' I've seen her and she looks more like a boiled lobster!

28.   He drinks rather a lot. He came in to have a blood test this morning—it's the first time I've seen a hypodermic syringe hiccup!

GOLFING

Here are a few thoughts on golfing, which may help you when compiling your speech.

1.   There are far too many jokes made about the clods turned up by golfers, and I'm surprised at the number of clods turned up here tonight.

2.   I am privileged to welcome any lady golfers that may have turned up, some of whom have handicaps, others very wisely left theirs waiting at the church.

3.   To any beginners I would say this . . . if the ball doesn't go in the direction you want it to, don't be discouraged, if it goes anywhere that's PRO-GRESS.

4.   Of course, there are always the diehards, men who say a woman's place is at the kitchen sink. A woman I know says she'll continue golf if it means taking the kitchen sink with her and judging by the weight of her bag I THINK SHE DOES.

5.   I'd like to bring a message of hope for those discouraged by the length of time it takes to complete the course . . . if the ranks of lady golfers continues

to swell, they're thinking of opening a beauty parlour on the 9th. Think of it, ladies . . . you can return to the clubhouse looking not a day older than when you started out.

6.   I'd like to pause here and explain a mystery that I know must be puzzling the ladies . . . you see, on a golf course men are heavy smokers and it is difficult to light a cigarette on a fairway in a high wind and THAT is the reason why you see men take a quick dive into the bushes! . . . Mind you, if they smoke much more, they'll have to wear wellington boots!

GOVERNMENT

1.   The Budget did one thing, it helped to stop all the smash-and-grab raids . . . I mean, with the price of petrol it's hardly worth it!

2.   The Government's talking about a National Lottery. Can you imagine it—Nationalised Bingo? The first one to shout 'House' gets a mortgage!

3.   The election time is coming. We'll all be getting the old promises . . . less hours, more money, nude bathing for unemployed, tenpin bowling for O.A.P.s and hairnets for pop groups.

4.   It's a frightening world. Russian leaders have only got to crack their knuckles and America might start firing back.

5.   Violence is getting worse. Last week there were 46 burglaries, 32 hold ups and 16 cosh bandits —and that was only in the House of Commons.

6.   The new symbol of the Tax Department is a brand new species of tropical plant—it's an out-stretched palm.

7.   Our local council's got a new panel game called Double Your Rates Money.

8.   I looked at the voting papers and I didn't know who to vote for so I made a block perm.

9.   When you think about voting, isn't it marvellous, you spend 18 years of your life learning to read and write—so that you can have the privilege of making a cross.

10.   Income Tax—the crowning insult is the envelope—right across the front is BLOOD DONORS URGENTLY NEEDED.

11.   The Government is spending a lot of money in research to prolong life because getting folk to live longer is the only possible way of getting more taxes out of them.

12.   If our local council sees smoke coming from your chimney they double your rates!

13.   Since the Budget I've been pleading with the bank manager to let me garage my car in the vault.

14.   I've just figured it out that success is a short circuit between the Mint and the Exchequer.

15.   I went into the House of Commons the other day to see them work—I watched them vote. It's really interesting, all the Labour Party go into one big lobby, all the Conservatives go into another big lobby . . . and all the Liberals get into a little tele-phone booth.

16.   Remember the young taxpayer of today is the old taxpayer of tomorrow.

17.   My great-grandfather was a politician, my grandfather was a politician, my father was a politician—and my son ain't gonna work either!

GUESTS

1.   Speaking of . . . (so and so) . . . which is something HE never fails to do.

2.   (reference to someone with large moustache and heavy sidewhiskers) . . . the ablution brush with skin.

3.   Nice fella . . . (so and so) . . . he has no favourites, JUST HATES EVERYBODY.

4.   (reference to a small man) . . . unfortunately he was run over by a Hoover.

5.   I don't know if we're supposed to thank . . . (so and so) . . . for his speech, personally I think he should thank us for listening.

6.   (reference to someone) . . . and I must say he looks well preserved. Perhaps a better word would be PICKLED.

7.   As I look around I see a lot of new faces . . . but mostly the old ones touched up.

8.   It's difficult to know what to say about our next guest—especially if you've had a very strict upbringing like myself. Anyway, he's just off to America. Some people go there for pleasure, some for business, in this case I think he's being deported.

C

9.   He's such a nice fellow. I knew him when he was popular.

10.   One thing about him, he always makes you feel at home, if that's any recommendation, because I've been to his place!

11.   I listened to the previous speaker and I think it was a marvellous achievement. It was a feat of mind over mutter.

HOLIDAYS

1.   The wife was going raving mad about wanting the sun and the soft sand, so I fixed her up nicely. It wasn't easy, but she'll soon settle down . . . IN THE FOREIGN LEGION!

2.   I had a happy week at the coast last year— LASHED TO A PIER. It was fun watching them all set fire to their deck-chairs to keep warm. I was lucky enough to attract the attention of a St. Bernard with a rescue rum.

3.   The secret of a good holiday is always the accommodation. My hotel was unique—it was banned by both the A.A. and the R.A.C.

4.   This is the place for me, I always come down here for a little peace . . . and there's some nice little pieces down here.

5.   Met a nice little piece yesterday—not what you'd call a raving beauty but then I didn't meet her under the best conditions—a lifeguard was giving her artificial respiration! She wasn't too happy

about that either—well, she was drinking a cup of coffee in a café at the time.

6.   You meet some queer characters at the seaside —one kept coming up behind my missus when she was in her bikini and pinching her seat! We wouldn't have minded but he was doing it with a pair of pliers!

7.   I had a different holiday this year. Well, the wife is fond of a little cove in Cornwall and I fancied a little peace in Wales and four of us had a marvellous, time.

8.   What a place . . . there was a black balloon hanging from the fireplace. I said, 'What's that for?' She said, 'It's Carnival Week.' It was so dark in there the bats were striking matches.

9.   I've had a lot of fun this summer around the coast—trying to keep warm. On one beach there was only two of us—me and a St. Bernard.

10.   Yesterday I met an American who's been over here for a fortnight on holiday. He was having a ride on a bus down Oxford Street. He told me he was thinking of staying another week and having a look at Regent's Street as well.

HOUSE

1.   Having trouble with the new house. I've got a nice piece of ground but I'm having trouble with the grass—three times this week I've had to mow the

hall. Talk about unseasoned timber, we've got a spiral staircase—mind you it was straight when we moved in, and the damp—well we don't bother with carpets . . . we've got fitted mildew. You think I'm kidding, even the roses on the wallpaper have got blight. Still I suppose we're lucky, at least the house is detached . . . well it wasn't until the house either side fell down.

2.   My house is so damp I've got the only fox terrier in the country that can quack!

3.   I wouldn't say the neighbours are nosey but all the knot holes in our fence have got eyelashes.

4.   There's one thing though, I do muck in with my neighbours. They throw muck in my garden and I throw muck in theirs.

5.   The houses these days are specially built for the modern climate—no foundations, just anchors!

6.   In our house we've got to the bare necessities and once your necessities are bare you can't invite mixed company, can you?

7.   The soil is so poor the worms are going around in gangs attacking the birds. Last week 14 greenfly died of malnutrition.

LADIES

1.   (reference to a much married woman) She had a nasty shock, they introduced her to a man she hadn't married.

2.   When she's got all her wedding rings on she looks like a curtain rod.

3.   She wakes up in the morning, looks across the pillow and doesn't know whether to say, 'Good morning', or 'Who are you?'

4.   She's got a standing order with her baker . . . one brown, one white and a wedding cake.

5.   She's been married for the umpteenth time, that's not bigamy, that's BLOODY MONOTONY!

6.   Ladies, remember when making your faces up, if you display the goods in the window . . . you must expect bargaining in the basement!

7.   Ladies . . . do remember, it's no use having 'come-to-bed' eyes, if you have a stay-in-the-kitchen body.

8.   In this modern age of cosmetics a woman can keep the bloom of youth in her cheeks . . . long after the cheeks of youth left her bloomers!

9.   Have you noticed the way some men stand up when a woman enters the room? It became popular round about the same time as the plunging neckline.

10.   She had a wart on the end of her nose but the doctor was very good, he gave her a bottle . . . it fitted right over it.

11.   I feel sorry for that girl; when she was in her teens she made a mistake. Anyone can make a mistake but this poor girl's paid for it—ever since, people have been staring at her and pointing her out. It seems that when she was 18 she grew a beard.

12.   She's got what they call Grecian features—looks like ARCHBISHOP MAKARIOS! She's still looking for a plastic surgeon who gives trading stamps!

13.   She's got a figure like a Volkswagen—all the weight's at the back.

14.   How about all this hairspray women keep using these days? I ran my face through one girl's hair and for two weeks my lips were glued to my nose.

15.   I gave my mother-in-law her favourite box of caramels—then I hid her teeth!

16.   She's certainly putting on a lot of weight. You can't tell if she's expanding or expecting.

17.   (about a film star) They've got a raffle on at the Customs to see who is going to search her.

18.   She said to me, 'I'm just a weak woman.' I said, 'That's fine, a week's plenty!'

19.   What a girl. Her shoulders were all white and creamy—it was just her face that was clotted.

20.   She always liked to dress like the film stars— in fact she was often mistaken for Edward G. Robinson.

21.   Four sisters got married at the same time and as they went into the church the organist played, 'Here Comes The Brood'.

22.   I must say she's a big woman—FAT! Every time she walks over a zebra crossing the stripes sag!

23.   When she goes for a holiday abroad she has to get a meat export licence.

24.   I've got an Eskimo pen friend—she's very affectionate, at the bottom of every letter she puts a row of noses!

25.   She once sent me a get well card three weeks before I was taken bad.

26.   She must have had a terrible nightmare— because I saw the hot water bottle running down the stairs screaming.

27.   She's got what you call a Pullman mouth— no lowers and very few uppers.

28.   I'm still trying to figure out if she's got bow legs or if she wears tight suspenders.

29.   Her father is a librarian and he's very strict with her. If you keep her out more than a week he fines you!

30.   She's so thin she can do the splits in a hobble skirt without stretching it.

31.   When I tell you she was fat . . . well last week she went to get some whalebone corsets made and they used up a whole whale.

32.   Her name was Blanche and when you look at her face it makes you!

33.   The poor girl in the Folies Bergère . . . she put a plaster on a pimple and they told her she was overdressed.

34.   Old lady to bus conductor . . . 'Am I all right for the British Museum?' He said, 'Yes, Madam, but I wouldn't leave it much longer.'

35.   Her father was so deaf he once conducted the family prayers while kneeling on the cat.

36.   Once upon a time you bought a little girl a doll's house and some candy—nowadays they want a flat and a packet of Marijuana.

37.   She certainly has the kind of face that all men go for—that's why they call her . . . Old Gopher Face!

38.   I wouldn't say she was a plain girl . . . but she's the only one I know who is grateful for smog!

39.   Her nose was more shiny than a Civil Servant's elbow.

40.   Saw a lovely girl at the swimming pool. She had lovely legs, pretty feet, ten toes, the same as any other girl, but she stood out in a crowd

because two were on one foot and all the rest were on the other.

41.   She said to me, 'Excuse me, have you got a light? Or do you know a better way to start a conversation?'

42.   Around her neck she still wears the fingermarks of her last husband.

43.   I saw this beautiful girl in the hotel passage —she cocked an eye at me and I cocked an eye at her . . . and we just stood there looking at each other —cockeyed!

44.   When the Mountains of Mourne swept down to the sea, they must have passed over her face.

45.   She said to me, 'Are you worrying about my age?' I said, 'Only the last two figures.'

46.   Some women have got dishpan hands, not her—she's got a dishpan face.

47.   I wouldn't say she was a good cook—she posted a recipe to a friend of hers and the pillarbox was sick.

48.   She wore a low cut gown—if it had been cut any lower the woman in the flat below could have been wearing it.

49.   Isn't it marvellous how women of 70 can manage to look 68?

50.   She looked into the wardrobe and said, 'What would you like me to change into?' I said, 'A woman.'

51.   What a smashing girl, what a figure—she could make the wool in a sweater look as if had never left the ball.

52.   She was a nice little thing, only four foot six—wide!

53.   She said, 'Do you like me the way I am?' I said, 'Yes, which way are you?'

54.   It was through Josephine that Napoleon used to stand with his hand tucked in his coat—he was keeping his hand on his wallet.

55.   She said to me, 'Do you like kissing?' I said, 'Yes, you know I do.' 'Well,' she said, 'you can kiss your car goodbye. I've just wrecked it.'

56.   She was so fat I danced with her for twenty minutes before I realised she was still sitting down.

57.   She said, 'Do you think I'm the right shape for a man?' I said, 'Yes, but you must remember you're a woman.'

58.   She kept pestering me for a mink outfit. So I gave her one—two guns and a trap.

59.   Big-busted women seem to be the thing in films these days. I saw two of them recently trying to get close enough together to shake hands. When they do get together, there's really a meeting of the Big Four.

60.   Aren't women funny? She's tried this new shiny make-up. Now her hanky doesn't know whether it's meant to blow or polish.

61.   She told me she saved up bundles of love letters—all tied up with blue ribbon. Poor old thing, she didn't know anybody well enough to post them to.

62.   She's a bit on the fat side. As I walked her home through the park one of her garters snapped and cut down four trees.

63.   You've heard of the living bra—hers has just died on her.

64.   She's what they call a sweater girl—and when I look at her I start to sweat.

65.   She looked like a million dollars—and you can imagine how lumpy a million dollars looks!

66.   What a figure—if it wasn't for the fact that she had housemaid's knees, she'd have had no shape at all.

67.   She said she wasn't hungry but it's the first time I've ever seen sparks come from a knife and fork.

68.   Did you hear about Raquel Welch? She fell asleep in the greenhouse—good job the sun went in!

69.   The poor girl was so bow-legged they hung her over the door for good luck!

70.   I kissed her right on the impulse and I said, 'I'll be frank with you, you're not the first girl I've kissed.' She said, 'I'll be frank with you—you've got a lot to learn.'

71.   She's got three sets of teeth, one upper, one lower and one mezzanine.

72.   She's a real landlady's daughter, got a heart of gold—yellow and hard.

73.   His wife is very charming—she came to meet me with outstretched curiosity. She said, 'Won't you come in for a bite?' So I went in and bit her. Then she made us a cup of Civil Servants—that's weak tea made in a strong bucket. She said, 'Will you have a biscuit? Or are your teeth broken already?'

74.   Frankly I don't remember how we met—I just sobered up and there she was.

75.   My mother-in-law came to see the fireworks. She doesn't usually keep late hours but unfortunately she stood too near the giant rocket and went up earlier than usual. She must have travelled a long

way—we haven't found her yet. Mind you, we haven't looked.

76.   She comes from a very wealthy family, her father's a head cashier on a bus!

77.   She was a bit on the fat side. Well, when I tell you she could ride a tandem and sit on both saddles at the same time. . . .

78.   She had her first beau when she was sixteen . . . 12 months later the other leg went.

79.   I took my mother-in-law down to the beach and we played burying each other in the sand. I must remember to go back next year and dig her up.

80.   I wouldn't say she was old, but if we all come from Adam and Eve she could have said goodbye personally.

81.   The poor girl was dieting and dieting, waiting for hips that never came in.

82.   Her mother's as fat as ever. If Shylock wanted his pound of flesh with her he could get it off one pimple.

83.   The film star's wedding cake. It was only 12 inches high but 18 foot long. It'll look all right on cinemascope.

84.   Still I don't care, I may be wrong, but I think she's beautiful and I think I'm wrong.

85.   I've tried everything with that girl, sweets, flowers, moonlight cruises—they all work.

86.   I remember the time she visited her Dad— she took him a pie she'd made with a file and a hacksaw inside it. Then, after he'd eaten those he beat the door down with the piecrust.

MISCELLANEOUS

1.   His name is a household word . . . like dustbin, or slop bucket!

2.   . . . went into a restaurant . . . must have been early, I got served the SAME DAY.

3.   And you've all heard of Van Gogh, he was the artist who lopped his lug 'ole off . . . then picked it up and said, 'WHAT'S THIS 'ERE?'

4.   . . . it's a bit like sex . . . when it's good it's wonderful, when it's bad . . . it's still pretty good.

5.   I was a bit worried when I saw the table laid, knife, fork and stomach pump.

6.   (kissing) It's what they call up-town shopping for down-town business.

7.   Take Nell Gwyn . . . and in her day most men DID . . . I'm not surprised King Charles kept cocker spaniels, he had to have one bitch he didn't buy presents for.

8.   I'd like to be Father Christmas just once . . . if only to see what a nudist hangs up to be filled.

9.   I remember when I was a kid . . . we had nothing to eat . . . nowhere to go . . . nothing to wear . . . THEN CAME THE DEPRESSION.

10.   I was the only kid in the street who had a gun that fired real bullets . . . after a week . . . I WAS THE ONLY KID ON THE STREET.

11.   I was never blessed with good looks . . . I was the only kid who had a pram with SHUTTERS ON.

12.   When I was born my father took one look at me, then ran like hell to Regent's Park and spent

the rest of the day throwing stones at the stork.

13.   When I was born I was so small my mother used to carry me around in her handbag . . . for the first two years of my life I thought my brother was a ball point pen! I was jealous of him because his top unscrewed!

14.   My brother used to walk about thinking he was a chicken . . . we'd have had him done away with . . . BUT WE NEEDED THE EGGS!

15.   I like a bubble car . . . if I can't park it . . . I PRICK IT!

16.   What about all this instant business? Instant tea, instant coffee, indigestion tablets for instant relief . . . EXLAX HAVE JUST FIRED THEIR RESEARCH CHEMIST.

17.   I suppose you've had a go at this striped toothpaste . . . makes quite a difference, especially if you've got STRIPED TEETH.

18.   We shall always find a reason to laugh— there's always hysteria!

19.   Joe says he's going to take it with him. I think he means it, he's just bought himself a fireproof money belt.

20.   He earns so much money he has to take in washing to pay his SURTAX.

21.   Frankly I don't know whether it's better to be a soldier fighting for freedom, or a civilian paying for democracy.

22.   This year hasn't started too good, all this working to rule and going slow. Even the bank robbers are cutting down to one a week.

23.   The show was so bad it's the first time I've ever heard the audience applaud the INTERVAL.

24.   I've just seen a poster that said Visit France. To make the poster look more attractive there was a picture of a girl in National Costume—bedroom slippers and a nightie.

25.   What about all this free gift business? One packet of soap powder, one plastic rose. I've got five rooms full of roses and a garage full of soap. I have to dig the car out.

26.   Wealthy . . . they've just paid over £90,000 for a painting. Well, it covers the damp patch on the wall.

27.   I know someone who goes to college, she's studying domestic science, with applied Psychology . . . and there's a double . . . a sort of how-do-you-like-your eggs—FREUD!

28.   He's a very modern vicar—he even wears a pair of stained-glass contact lenses.

29.   I saw a burglar climbing out of the window, the occupier grabbed one of his legs and a police-man outside grabbed him by the other and all the damn fool could shout was, 'Quick, someone—MAKE A WISH!'

30.   How can a pot look so good on a belly dancer and so bad on me?

31.   Some people were upset at not being invited to the wedding. I wasn't even invited to the divorce!

32.   Do you remember the good old days, when beer foamed and dish-water didn't?

33.   I'm not getting any laughs with this material but the smiles are deafening.

34.   I love this new idea of chocolates that print he flavours on the lid. Now you can get eyestrain and tooth decay at the same time.

35.   They've all got colds in my house. I had cereal for breakfast this morning and even that was going Snap, Crackle, Sniff!

36.   Monologue:

As you're strolling along life's highway,
Do friends smile at you when you've passed?
They do . . . then check your elastic.
You're wearing your bloomers half mast!

37.   I said, 'Doctor, can you tell me what this lump is on my back?' He said, 'Take your clothes off.' Then after a while, he said, 'How long have you left school?' I said, 'About 19 years.' He said, 'Did you ever wonder what happened to your satchel?'

38.   I love the way I was greeted when I arrived. They all rushed out and shook me warmly by the throat!

39.   I like my job—apart from anything else you meet such interesting money.

40.   It's getting so that a woman's nightmare these days is when she can't do the top button of her blouse up.

41.   They're very narrow-minded in that household—I saw two flies walk up the mirror with their eyes closed.

42.   Fellow crossed a sheep with a kangaroo and got a woolly jumper.

43.   I remember when I was young I was very poor and I couldn't afford anything. I thought, I'll work hard and be successful and I did just that. For years and years I worked hard and became amous and then came the time when I could really afford those big steaks. Trouble is, now I can afford those big steaks, I've got no bloody teeth.

44.   We've given up using coal at home—it's too expensive. We're burning genuine Chippendale logs!

45.   Coming from a poor family we could only afford one meal a day—it seemed to split the family into three groups. The quick—the strong . . . and the starving!

46.   My Mum says that my Dad was the nicest man she'd ever met. In fact she'd like to meet him again.

47.   I was the intelligent one—when I was nine I could go to the psychiatrist all by myself.

48.   I always thought that boiled ham was an actor with sunstroke.

49.   Life used to be hard in my young days—they couldn't get a family allowance for me—so they stuck me in the window and took a collection.

50.   The vicar said to me, 'Stay away from girls, or you'll be earning the wages of sin.' I said, 'Maybe . . . but look at the pay packet!'

51.   I had a hell of a job getting here. I travelled through the whole of the night and if you happen to see a night with a hole in it, that's the one I came through.

52.   I could do with a good tonic. I don't know whether to have a few days in Paris or join the Luton Girls' Choir.

53.   I had a terrible accident last week. I introduced a sailor to a blonde and didn't hop out of the way in time.

54.   Pardon me, Comrade, what's the time by your bomb?

55.   With a face like his (hers) he/she could go

places . . . The Zoo, Holloway, Chamber of Horrors
. . .

56.   I must have looked very ill—I handed the prescription over to the chemist and he gave me a harp!

57.   I bet I'm the only fellow with an overdraft at the Blood Bank.

58.   I was a lovely baby—when I was six months old I had little pink cheeks and when I was eight months old I had big red cheeks . . . and when I was ten months old my mother loosened my binder.

59.   I had a terrible great boil on the back of my neck, the doctor tried to lance it—twice he fell off his horse.

60.   Observation made during a dock strike. It's a kind of shame, seeing all that food lying around the docks where people can't get at it—it ought to be in the shops, where people can't afford it.

61.   If you think my eyes are bloodshot, you should see them from this side.

62.   I come from a small village, nobody ever buys any papers there—you know what everybody else is doing. You buy a paper once in a while, just to see if they got caught at it.

63.   Pal of mine's rolling in money, he's got his own business—knife grinding in Soho!

64.   I've got a good doctor—he's promised me that if my arm doesn't set straight, he's going to break the other one to match!

65.   I had a shock yesterday . . . I was walking down Oxford Street and I bumped into an Englishman!

66.   He gave a performance that tore their hearts

D

out—it didn't do their stomachs any good either.

67.   I was sitting in the front room with my girl friend and her father came in and said, 'Can I watch you two, there's nothing on T.V.?'

68.   I'm unlucky—if they sawed a woman in half I'd get the half that eats!

69.   I'm just plain unlucky—if I was Anne Boleyn and I pulled a cracker, six to four I'd get a paper hat!

70.   I've just come from a Government building —you know, where you get all your licences under one roof. A long counter and a lot of little pigeon holes, Marriage Licence, Driving Licence, Dog Licence, Building Licence. I wanted a wireless licence. I must have gone to the wrong hole—you are now looking at Cocker Spaniel Number 42670.

71.   The doctor's a bit queer, every time he brings out his stethoscope he looks at you and says, 'Toss you for ends.'

72.   The psychiatrist asked me about my nerves. He said, 'Tell me, do you jump in the evening when your wife breaks the silence?' I said, 'What silence?'

73.   I said, 'My nerves are in a shocking state, doctor. I don't know how I can go on facing my audience.' He said, 'What puzzles me is how they've gone on facing you.'

74.   Spring is on the way. That's the time when young couples start doing in the open what they've been practising all the winter in the pictures.

75.   They bought a large T.V. set. The only place big enough to stand it was inside her mouth.

76.   They had twin boys, Amos and Andy. They would have been christened Albert and Fred but the vicar was wearing dark glasses.

77.   This give-away idea is getting well out of hand. Things are getting so bad now that if you save the tops from every pound packet of rice they send you a free bridesmaid.

78.   Never put off till tomorrow what you can do today because there might be a law against it by then.

79.   It must be terrible to be so unpopular that when you look in the mirror the reflection holds its nose.

80.   It's about as scarce as a taxi driver giving road signals.

81.   They're a fastidious couple—she's fast and he's hideous.

82.   She's been a Civil Servant for so long even the lines on her face are dotted.

83.   I went into a pub for a drink and a man came up to me and said, 'Do you like darts?' I said 'Yes.' He said, 'Good, I've just thrown one in your back.'

84.   London's a crazy place. A man rushed up to me and said, 'Have you ever wanted to dial 999?' I said, 'Yes.' 'Well,' he said, 'you've got a fine excuse in a minute, this is a stick-up!'

85.   I was different from the rest of the family, I only had one head.

86.   When I was naughty my mother used to box my ears and I used to go mad when I couldn't find the box.

87.   The film I saw was really different, it had a surprise ending. The manager of the cinema rushed down the gangway and shot two of his usherettes.

88.   The wicked price of coal—anthracite £9 a

ton. I know a shop where they're selling it—in packets of 20.

89.   Spring—that's when a young man's fancy turns . . . and runs off with some other perisher.

90.   I've eaten so much starchy food lately my skin keeps itching and I break out in laundry marks.

91.   I've learned a trick from the Americans—never get married until you've saved enough for the divorce.

92.   You know what the wolf whistle is? If you get the wolf whistle it means you've got IT . . . and if you're a man it means a haircut and a change of walk.

93.   What a reception they gave me—what a welcome! I'll always carry the scars to remember it by.

94.   Here's a marvellous way of keeping warm on 1 cwt of coal—gallop round the garden with it on your back!

95.   I said to the girl behind the counter in the shop—'Come round the corner for a bite?' She said, 'The manager's out—bite me here.'

96.   You fellows want to box clever like me. I never go home with hairs on my collar—my girl friends are bald.

97.   Surplus rolling stock is an overflow from a corset.

98.   My first race was the relay race. You know, where they pass that long thin thing to each other . . . and that's what I was—the long thin thing.

99.   I took up swimming and became a coast-guard—I was no different from any other coastguard except that girls shouted for help *after* the rescue.

100.   Don't you love the reception some people give you? Such as, 'Are you staying, or shall I open a window?'

101.   In Russia it's fair shares for all and if you take your share and make money with it, they stick you up against a wall and shoot the 'share' right out of you.

102.   I shall never forget my dear old mother's words the day they sent me to prison. She just looked up and said, 'Hello son!'

103.   He's very swift on his feet. He got that way through being a member of a nudist camp close to an airfield.

104.   It's coming to something these days in the cinemas. Nowadays they're showing films where you have to show a National Health card before you can get in.

105.   I've just seen the latest thing in sleeping pills, the new kind, you get three. You don't have to swallow them, you take them up to bed and juggle with them.

106.   Have you tried the new confidence pills? Confidence pills is right. I lifted the lid and there they were—fighting each other.

107.   It was certainly a severe winter. My doctor thinks so too. Over his mantelpiece he's got a picture of Stag at Bay and that's had the flu twice.

108.   I'm all set for the Spring. I've bought an after-shave lotion called Desire, a haircream called Temptation and there's a van coming in the morning with a new couch!

109.   I've invented a new idea for getting stains out of tablecloths—it's called a pair of scissors.

110.   Did you hear about the two centipedes standing in a front garden and a beautiful blonde centipede walked past? One said to the other, 'Look at that smashing pair of legs, pair of legs, pair of legs, pair of legs, pair of legs.'

111.   Have you seen the latest thing in women's clothing? MEN.

112.   When I opened the door there was a tramp standing there. He asked if I would give him something for the road, so I gave him my old army boots!

113.   They met me at the station—they said, 'Did you eat on the way up?' I said, 'No.' They said, 'Well, never mind, you'll get another chance on the way back.'

114.   I remember a school pal of mine—we had a tiff one day and I tipped him head first into a bucket of cement. He stayed like it—mind you I wouldn't have known if I hadn't received a letter from him on House of Commons notepaper.

115.   It's a poor look-out for any man who hasn't been Barbara Hutton's (or any much married woman's) husband.

116.   And what about the price of phone calls? You lift up the receiver now they don't say, 'Can I help you?' They say, 'Can you afford it?'

117.   In the old days a footpad would knock you down and leave you there. Today, if a fellow coshes you, at least he kicks your ribs in to take your mind off it.

118.   That American imported coal is the stuff—they call it pure coal. It doesn't smoke, it doesn't go out, it just lays in the grate blowing bubble gum.

119.   I did a silly thing, I bought a giant Catherine

Wheel, what a size! I nailed it to the garage door and now I'm the only bloke in our street with a revolving garage.

120.   The next-door neighbour has just bought a dog—it's a lovely big thing, very fond of children. The trouble is it ate four before they found out.

121.   Whatever happens, I believe in keeping a stiff upper lip. Believe me it does something for you—it makes you talk funny like this.

122.   When they deliver those whacking great sacks of coal, there's no heat in them. It's the little envelope with the bill in that makes you sweat.

123.   I went to a boarding school—it was different from kindergarten. I studied my new teacher's legs for three weeks and then somebody told me she was a man.

124.   I used to spend all my money on sweeties, blondes, brunettes . . .

125.   I went into the milking shed . . . saw a chap sitting there gazing at the cows. I said, 'Is anything wrong?' He said, 'No, I'm a psychiatrist and it's a rare treat to spend an hour with a bunch of contented females.'

126.   I knew I was different from other children the third time my mother pinned a nappy round my face.

127.   When I was born my father laughed loud and long. He wanted to drown the noise of the gunshot.

128.   It was difficult for the doctor to examine me, every time he put the stethoscope to my chest it overlapped. He couldn't inoculate me either—the needle was thicker than my arm.

129.   My parents dropped me on my head on purpose—they were trying to get a better shape.

130.   The baby has drunk so much orange juice they don't change it, they peel it.

131.   Telephone charges are going up again and just as they've started the new weather service—that means by the time you've phoned them twice you could have paid for a raincoat!

132.   Two brooms in a cupboard, a female broom and a male broom, and the female broom said, 'Do you know, I think I'm going to have a new bristle?' The male broom said, 'That's impossible, dear, we haven't swept together for years.'

133.   A fellow came out of the hotel and shouted at a uniformed man whom he thought to be the commissionaire. 'Hey, my man, call me a taxi!' The uniformed man scowled and replied, 'Do you mind, I'm an Admiral in the British Navy.' The man said, 'O.K., call me a battleship.'

134.   Just as the man was knocked flying by a taxi the driver called, 'Look out!' The man on the road replied, 'Why—are you coming back?'

MUSIC

1.   Mind you, I found piano lessons exciting, I used to sit there, running my fingers up and down. Then the music mistress said, 'That was wonderful . . . NOW TRY IT ON THE PIANO!'

2.   What a marvellous band. I don't know them

all but there's three on trumpet, four on trombone, two on National Assistance and five on probation.

3. I could have been a great musician. But what can you play on a grate?

4. My father was musical too, he had harmoniums, harpsichords, guitars and the biggest lyre in the world—ME.

5. I learned to play the bagpipes and you know what the bagpipes are—a sort of an octopus with rigor mortis.

6. What a voice—he's the only singer I know who ever got an answer from Chloe!

7. I went to a concert last night and there was a fellow singing the Song of the Flea. The audience didn't applaud, they were too busy scratching.

8. There was a four-piece band swinging in the corner. I got there just in time to cut them down.

9. What a combination, flute, oboe and slop bucket.

10. If music is the food of love—she's a 32 bar rest.

11. A fine musician but he came to a sad end, he played the clarinet, tried to play a B Sharp above a Top C and disappeared up his own glockenspiel.

12. My brother and I led a humdrum life— he hummed, I drummed.

13. My music teacher said, 'You don't practise the piano like any normal boy.' Then she slammed the lid down and broke three of my toes.

14. Two men served in the Army in India together and met many years later in England. After the usual welcome one said, 'What are you doing these days?' The other replied, 'Well, you know I

D*

was in the band? I played the violin, married a woman who plays the piano, and I've got a lovely daughter who's very good with the cello. You must come round one night and we'll give you a musical evening.' The other replied, 'Yes, as a matter of fact, I won the All Army Boxing Championships, married a policewoman and my daughter has just won the Black Belt at Judo. You must come round to us one night—we can't give you a musical evening, but we'll give you a BLOODY GOOD HIDING.'

PLACES

1.   (of a place) It's so exclusive, if the toilet is engaged they announce it in *The Times*!

2.   It's a tough neighbourhood, even the churches are locked up. If you want to pray you have to go round to the back door, knock three times and say, 'Peter sent me.'

3.   I stayed at the Station Hotel—that was a mistake—I couldn't wash my hands for a fortnight!

4.   I stayed at a very nice boarding house and the rules were very strict, the front door was locked at 10 o'clock every night. Three times I had to come down at midnight to let the landlady in.

5.   I stayed at a nice little place—it was right near the sea. The only trouble was, when the tide went out it took the furniture with it.

6.   There were three kinds of water pipes there, one for hot, one for cold and one to bang on when there's no hot or cold water!

7.   What a hotel! They don't fold the blankets—they chase them out of the room with a D.D.T. spray.

8.   The hotel . . . have I got a room? Frankly I'm not sure, the only way to get in that room is to be born there. Every time I swallow, my Adam's Apple pushes the window up!

9.   Their house is so big there's a bathroom on the way to the bathroom in case you're in a hurry.

10.   It was a nice hotel and then the maid came in to see if I wanted anything—I looked at her and decided I didn't.

11.   I had lovely accommodation. I remember one place, a grey-haired old lady answered the door. She said, 'Are you one of those people who indulge in late parties and drinking and dancing till all hours?' I said, 'No.' She said, 'Well I hope I don't disturb you, because I do.'

12.   I sat down to have something to eat and the dog growled at me. I said, 'What's the matter with him?' She said, 'Don't take any notice, you've got his plate.' I said, 'Well, I hope he makes friends.' She said, 'So do I, you're sleeping with him.'

13.   But he was a nice dog, we made friends. In the morning he brought me some bones and laid them at my feet. Then I looked down and found they were my feet.

14.   The room was so small I daren't brush my teeth sideways—I'd have knocked both neighbours up.

15.   The hotel was so old it's the only place I know where you sign the register with a hammer and chisel!

16.   There was a dreadful noise yesterday when something fell down the stairs—it was my bedroom!

17.   I hadn't been in the hotel room ten minutes when the maid came up. She said, 'I've come to turn your bed down.' I said. 'I've already turned it down, I'm sleeping on the floor.'

18.   They've got a lovely old home and I do mean old—half the time you're there you don't know whether you're a guest or a prop!

19.   I stayed at a lovely little hotel, right next to the Splendid. Mine was called the Sordid.

THE PRESS

1.   Journalism isn't everybody's meat . . . there are still people who prefer to work!

2.   (of a critic) . . . He's given us some of the best JEERS of his life.

3.   (journalist) A bundle of hay in the field of literature.

4.   . . . keeps a spare wardrobe for his libel suits.

5.   Newspapers have a great tradition behind them . . . from the very beginning they were the means of spreading news quickly . . . THEN CAME WOMEN.

6.   He writes for three papers . . . Daily . . . Sunday and IZAL.

7.   Such great changes in the newsprint world . . . newspapers amalgamating with each other. I can't

wait for the *News of the World* to amalgamate with the *Sunday Mirror* . . . just think . . . PICTURES AS WELL!

THE SERVICES

1. Believe me, when I left the Services I left with regret—I was sorry I'd ever been in.

2. My old Dad was a pioneer in the world of Aviation. I shall never forget the time he lashed an old basket to a balloon—she screamed the place down!

3. I was in the R.A.F. for a while—I got drummed out for throwing potatoes into jet engines and spraying the airfield with chips.

4. I'll never forget the first time I flew a plane—when I landed the thing I made a perfect landing, right in the middle of the runway. There was only one thing wrong—it was a seaplane!

5. I know one R.A.F. Officer, he stitched his wings on his tunic upside down—took off and flew straight down a rabbit hole.

6. And then there's the Navy, they've all got bell bottoms—don't half make a noise when they sit down. Those tattoos—they're so realistic. One fellow had a palm tree tattooed on his chest—the M.O. kicked him in the ribs and three coconuts fell off.

7. I said when I arrived I was proud to see the flag flying from the mast. He said. 'Don't worry, it'll fly back again when you've gone.'

8.　　Do you know that ignorance still exists in the Army—even below the rank of Sergeant? In fact there are still men who think that a palliasse is a friendly donkey.

9.　　I was in a tough mob—our trumpeter used to blow Reveille from an armoured car.

10.　　I was in a mixed unit in the Army. Every morning the bugler came out and instead of blowing Reveille, he blew two choruses of 'Come Out Come Out Wherever You Are'.

11.　　The bugler came to a very sad end, poor fellow. He blew the Last Post outside the Battersea Dogs' Home.

12.　　Sergeants are like race horses—once the tapes go up there's no holding them.

13.　　I remember Catterick—the days of the gay 90s. Ninety days for this, ninety days for that.

14.　　I've been looking at the Navy's might—I've an idea some of the Wrens might too.

15.　　The Captain ran up a string of flags—took us an hour to get him down again.

TELEVISION

1.　　Happy days . . . it's all changed now. Of course the 'telly's' done that, it's all sex and violence every time you switch on . . . and then, of course, there's the ADULT PROGRAMMES!

2.　　The Russians are beginning to like our programmes. Their favourite programme over there is Comrade Perry Mason. They love him—if he loses a case they SHOOT THE JUDGE!

3. I saw a musical on T.V. the other night. I don't know how far back they went for that one but Sybil Thorndyke was in the chorus!

4. I love those adverts on the television . . . 'Is your hair coming out in handfuls? If you look as if you've been waylaid by an Apache—you forgot to massage with Scalpo. Remember it comes in three strengths—Tufty—Shaggy—and . . . WHICH WAY TO THE SHEEP DIP.'

5. There are so many doctors and surgeons on the television these days. Last week I watched one of them take an appendix out for the third time, which was very impressive, but I'd like to meet the guy who keeps putting it back!

6. We don't have television at home—we're still trying to get something good on radio!

7. You should see me with television. I sit in front of the set all night long—can't get away from it. I'm afraid someone might switch it on.

8. (announcement on television) We apologise to the television viewers in the Holme Moss area, who, owing to a fault at the transmitter, have had the sides of their houses blown in.

9. Isn't progress wonderful? I've just seen a can of beans advertising television!

10. I've got a new television set—a 47 inch screen! It's very nice, the only thing is if you've got a nice supper laid out on the table you have to keep pushing the actors back in the set.

THOUGHTS ON LIFE

1.   Today and tonight is a sandwich—it's up to you what you put into it.

2.   Good manners are a very valuable asset—they are like the hallmark on precious metal.

3.   Laughter to life is like salt to a meal—pass the cruet.

4.   Life is a cake—share it with someone before it gets stale.

5.   Each day is a day worth trying.
       To achieve an impossible plan,
       So don't say you wouldn't, or couldn't,
         or shouldn't
       It may just turn out that YOU CAN!

6.   If someone says something to please you,
       And with pleasure your ears gently burn,
       Why not try to go just one better,
       And DO something nice in return!

7.   It's the women of the world who teach the babies to toddle . . . Then the men take over and show them how to march . . . TO WAR.

8.   Remember that there is no rebate to life,
       Not for one single moment you live,
       So why not enjoy what there is to enjoy,
       And forgive what there is to forgive.

9.   An imperfect friend is of far more value than a perfect stranger.

10.   Dawn and sunset are the goal posts of each day—don't worry about the score, have a good game.

11.   The distance between you and companionship is only a handshake away.

TRANSPORT

1.   You have to wait a long time for a bus these days. You'd think they'd come a long way—when you see the colour of the conductor you realise they have. No wonder they're late—they stop every half hour for a curry break!

2.   Faster trains don't suit everyone. The way I look at it is this, it all depends on whether the mother-in-law is coming or going!

3.   They are more careful now on the railways, if you send a parcel they don't throw it about—not until they've bashed it with a hammer to see if it's breakable!

4.   I was in the Lost Property Office and a woman came in. She said to the man, 'Have you seen my umbrella?' He said, 'No,' so she showed it to him.

5.   Railway men are going to work to rule—I'm glad they told us because we'd never have noticed.

6.   The plane started twisting and turning in all directions. The hostess said, 'Don't be alarmed, the pilot's just taken his medicine and forgotten to shake the bottle.'

7.   He's worked so long on the underground trains that his eyelids open and shut sideways.

8.   Three hooligans (ton-up boys) walked into a café and started to insult a little lorry driver and although they kept it up for some time the lorry driver said nothing. They did their best to provoke him but he would have none of it. After a while the lorry driver paid the waitress and left whereupon the three louts said to the girl, 'Not much of a man, is

he?' She replied, 'Not much of a driver either, he's just run over your three motor bikes.'

9.   It's good to be here. I came by train from Manchester—well, I had three or fours days to kill.

WEATHER

1.   The weather doesn't help . . . so changeable. Yesterday an old lady collapsed with the heat—by the time they picked her up, she'd died of FROST-BITE!

2.   Last year was the worst for weather, it must have been; three blokes jumped off the Air Ministry roof. Mind you they did it properly . . . in formation!

3.   What a winter we've had—and the price of things!—it cost me a fortune for fires. I got one bill for £8 and that was only for MATCHES!

4.   We certainly can't grumble at the summer we've had. Last week it was so hot I passed a field of cows, all lying on their backs giving themselves a milk shake. All except one—she let fly with two quarts of steam!

5.   It's sad about the weather forecaster who was so depressed he went out and shot himself—with a water pistol.

6.   Last night was the coldest night and I know that's a fact because yesterday I built a snowman in the garden and at three o'clock this morning it knocked on the back door and asked if it could stand in the hall for five minutes.

7.   The woman next door hung her washing out in all that snow. Half an hour later her husband's underpants crawled back under the door and stood with their backs to the fire.

8.   It must have been cold last night, my hot water bottle broke out in goose pimples.

9.   The cold weather doesn't worry me—you're now looking at the only man in the country with a pair of Davy Crockett underpants. I was walking around with a big grin on my face . . . I'd forgotten to cut the tail off!

10.   The weather was so bad I was woken up one night by seagulls tapping on the window—asking to come in.

THE WIFE

1.   I proposed to her in the Ladies Excuse Me and after that she won the Spot Prize. She should have done, she was covered in 'em.

2.   Then she took me to meet her parents. Real earthy people. Her father had a fine old country seat —you could tell that by looking at his fine old country trousers. We came down to a typical farm-house tea—a pint mug and a drop scone. I didn't bother with the scone—I saw where they dropped it. Every year they have a Sports Day on the Village Green. Her mother won the high jump—I don't think she would have done, but she backed into the javelin thrower. Very confusing for the vicar—he

was judging some autumn bloomers when she flew over his head. We were to have had Morris Dancing —but Morris couldn't get his boots on.

3.   I don't know why I keep torturing myself but I remember our wedding. It was a cautious affair— she said, 'I will,' I said, 'I might,' and it turned out WE DIDN'T!

4.   My wife is a little different—she's like a politician—sits up in the house all night asking awkward questions!

5.   My missus is very unlucky, she can't stand water. She even gets seasick in a launderette. I think it springs from her childhood. It could have been they used boiling water at her christening! Her brother loves water—in fact he's just got a job as a lifeguard in a car wash!

6.   The bride looked lovely in the twenty-foot train of white veiling—my missus had a similar outfit but she looked more like a side of bacon in a deep freeze!

7.   I shall never forget my wedding—the ceremony took so long, had to stop twice for a shave— not me—the bride!

8.   I've just bought her mother a lovely chair. The only trouble is it's a bit heavy on electricity!

9.   To me she's like the girl from the house next door, not like my wife—she just looks like the house next door!

10.   The wife came up here in the car with me, she moaned all the way . . . in the end I had to let her out of the boot!

11.   Women are funny things—take my wife, she's been very miserable lately, very upset, I think she's

teething . . . well not exactly teething, they keep slipping out.

12.   My wife is a real blue-blood—she's just given a transfusion to a fountain pen.

13.   Then there's her mother, well her face is her fortune—it should be kept in a vault. She'll never live to be as old as she looks.

14.   I'm having a little trouble with the girl friend—she can't get on with the wife. I'm not surprised—neither can I.

15.   Had a nasty bump in the car outside my house—you never heard such a crash. The wife heard it, she came running out of the house, poor thing—she was trembling so much she could hardly hold the insurance policy.

16.   She's just got her new set of National Health teeth. They're real smashers—they'll go through anything—I think they're off a gear wheel.

17.   Then the wife came in, looking rather different than usual. I said, 'Darling, you've found a new beauty treatment.' She said, 'Beauty treatment nothing, I've just been run over.'

18.   I don't regret being married for one moment. Mind you, apart from that one moment I hate every minute of it.

19.   The wife was ironing her brassière and I said, 'I don't know why you bother. You've got nothing to put in it.' She said, 'So . . . I iron your pants!'

20.   Last year my wife made a resolution never to go through my pockets again and I made a resolution never to set mousetraps in them. I broke my resolution—she broke all her fingers.

21.   When I saw her dressed up in her bridal gown I realised what her mother meant when she said she was getting rid of a white elephant.

22.   I've been happily married for years and here's the snag—the wife comes out next Friday.

23.   I wouldn't have married her, only her father promised to settle something on me—I didn't know he meant his relations. Relations!—when I carried my bride over the threshold it took me three days to get to the fireplace.

24.   Last week my wife lost a stone—can't understand it, I tied it as tight as I could.

YOUNGER GENERATION

1.   Did you read about the young kid of 15 who went to its mother and said, 'Now that I'm fifteen, can I wear lipstick, mascara, high heels and nylon stockings?' Fifteen! ! The mother said, 'Certainly not, GEORGE!'

2.   These days the kids have got the money— well, they need it with the price of hairdos, lipsticks, mascara, eyeshadow . . . and it's just as expensive for THE GIRLS!

3.   What about the new fashions? We don't have to look to knees any more now, it's NAVELS!

4.   Kids are getting married earlier every year, aren't they? Before long they'll be going straight from Sunday School and up the aisle. Vicars won't

know whether to marry them or hold them over the font!

5.   Some of them even have trial marriages these days. I don't know, they'll be wanting Green Shield Stamps with it next!

6.   I'm not knocking modern singers. Anyone who can turn adenoids into money earns my respect.

7.   Teenagers are so advanced these days. I saw their version of Cinderella—they didn't use a slipper, they used a bra!

8.   I know a twelve-year-old whose hair is turning prematurely green!

9.   I can remember the Twist (or modern dance) when it had a different name—the D.T.s.

10.   I know a teenager who's been wearing stretch pants for three years. This morning she tried to stand up without them and couldn't.

11.   I know a rock singer who sings so badly he even snaps his fingers off-key!

12.   To dance these days the modern way, you have to be young, athletic, uninhibited and it helps if one leg is longer than the other!

13.   Modern dancing seems rather strange. I can remember when the fellows who did it weren't dancing—they were trying to get out of the Army.

14.   These skinheads have their hair cut so short —there's only one trouble, they have to keep their dandruff in their wallet!

15.   I have been visiting one of these new progressive schools—you know, where the porter meets the boys and says, 'Carry your cosh, sir?'

16.   I was speaking to the headmaster. I said, What do you think of this self-expression theory,

allowing the boys to do as they please?' He said, 'See those two jars of ash on the mantelpiece? They're my last two schools!'

LONGER STORIES

1.   . . . old lady who went with her friend to the Police Station to report that her husband was missing and the Police Sergeant said, 'Well, tell me, what does he look like? Give us a description of him.' The woman said, 'Well, he's 29 years old and he's 6ft 2ins, and he's dark and he's handsome.' Her friend said, 'Wait a minute, your old man's bald, fat, and fifty.' She said, 'I know, but who wants *him* back?'

2.   There were two workmen on top of a house, taking off the paint with a blowlamp and the foreman called up from the street below. He said, 'Jack,' and the one with the blowlamp turned round to look down and the flame of the blowlamp was playing on his mate's ear. His mate didn't say anything for a minute and then suddenly he looked up and said, 'Blimey, Jack, somebody ain't 'alf talking about me.'

3.   My little boy came home the other day with his trousers all torn. His mother took them off to sew them up and sent him to bed. Later we heard a scuffling in the cellar, so she called down, 'Are you running about down there with no trousers on?' and the answer came back, 'No, ma'am, I'm just emptying the gas meter.'

4.   Miss Brightwell joined the Golf Club and

they were rather snooty at the Golf Club. Miss Brightwell bounced into the locker room, wanted to make friends and started to tell the girls some saucy stories. When she'd gone out to do some practise shots the Captain, who was very snooty, said to the girls, 'How dare that new member come in here telling us filthy stories? The next time she does a thing like that I expect you girls to say nothing and walk out of the room.' So Miss Brightwell flounced back in after she'd done some practise shots and as she was getting her jumper off she said, 'I say, girls, have you heard, all the prostitutes are going to Vietnam to entertain the troops?' There was a deathly silence and they all slowly started to walk towards the door and Miss Brightwell said, 'Well, don't hurry girls—the boat doesn't go till Thursday.'

5.   They hadn't been married long when he had to go away, so he took her to see him off at the station. When the guard blew the whistle he bent down to kiss her and his top teeth came loose. Now he didn't know whether to leave his teeth and kiss the miss, or fix his teeth and miss the kiss. It was a very awkward situation. He didn't want to miss the kiss, although he knew he would miss the miss, but while he was messing about like this, he made a silly mistake and kissed the train just as it went. Well you can imagine this upset the miss, I mean the misfortune is this, she missed the kiss, he missed the train and his teeth are still missing.

6.   Ah, what it is to be married! I come home every night from a hard day at the office to a beautiful, warm, comfortable flat. My wife is waiting to hand me my slippers and the evening paper. Then

she runs out to the kitchen and cooks me a luscious
dinner and after that she puts me in my easy chair
by the fire and hands me my pipe—then she washes
the dishes. Finally, she comes and snuggles down
at my side and starts to talk and talk and she talks
and talks and I wish she'd drop dead.

7.   Don't look so depressed, there's only two
things in life to worry about, either your health is
good, or it isn't. If it's good, then there's nothing to
worry about, if it isn't, there's two things to worry
about, either you'll live or you won't. If you live,
there's nothing to worry about and if you don't,
there's only two things to worry about, either you'll
go to heaven or the other place. If you go to heaven
you've got nothing to worry about and if you go to
the other place you'll be so damn busy shaking
hands with old friends you won't have time to
worry.

8.   A village vicar, having to go to London for a
few days, left instructions for a biblical quotation to
be painted on a big board and hung over the church
hall. While he was away his instructions were lost
and dutifully they wired him in London for further
instructions and for the text as follows:

Please advise text and dimensions.

The poor girl behind the counter in the Post Office
nearly fainted when the vicar handed his telegram
in, it read:

Unto us a son is born 8 feet long and 3 feet wide.

9.   A young lady walked into a public house and
a young gentleman, wishing to be friendly, said,
'Are you going to have one?' She replied, 'No, it's
just the way my coat's buttoned!'

10. What appeared to be a young French nurse-maid pushing a pram was duly admired by a passing gentleman. He beamed at the bonnie baby, then raised his hat to the nursemaid and said, 'Parlez vous Français?' She said, 'No, Chevrolet coupé, Epping Forest.'

11. A fellow rushed into the Roman Catholic Church and dashed into the Confessional Box. He banged on the wall and very urgently said, 'I've got a confession to make. I've committed a Cardinal Sin . . . last night I had six women.' A quiet voice was heard to say, 'Are you married, my son?' He said, 'I'm not even a Roman Catholic but I had to tell somebody.'

12. First prostitute to second prostitute, 'If I'm not in bed by eleven o'clock tonight, I'm packing up and going home.'

13. A Bunny Girl wanted to get married in her Bunny costume. She got as far as the Church when the vicar barred her way. 'You're not coming in here dressed like that,' he said. The girl replied, 'Why not? I've got a Divine right.' Whereupon the vicar said, 'You've got a smashing left as well, but you're still not coming in here like that.'

14. Two sailors going home on leave in a train, and the only other occupant of the carriage was a young vicar. There was silence as they all read their papers. Suddenly one sailor looked up and said to his mate, 'Joe, what are you going to do when you go home on leave?' Joe said, 'I'm going up to the pub, have a few beers, go to the dogs, see a few races, chase a few women,' and the vicar was heard to go 'Tut, tut, tut.' A little while later the other one

looked up and said, 'What are you planning to do, Harry?' Harry said, 'I shall go to Epsom, see a few races, one or two night clubs and chase a few birds,' and the vicar was heard again to 'Tut, tut, tut.' Silence reigned for a while and then suddenly the first sailor looked up and said, 'Joe, what's lumbago?' Whereupon the vicar jumped in sharply and said, 'Lumbago, my son, is a very serious illness, which comes from drinking, gambling and staying out late at night chasing women.' The sailor said, 'Oh, thanks, mate—only I see the Bishop of London's got it.'

15.   An old spinster was frustrated. She took her two parrots in a cage down to the vet and said, 'Can you tell me which one of these birds is the male?' He said, 'Madam, there's a very simple way of finding out. Take both birds home in the cage, stand it on the table, put a large cloth round it, switch out the light and wait for the scuffle. When you hear a scuffle, put your hand inside quickly and grab the aggressive bird—that'll be the male.' The dear old lady did exactly as he told her. She stood the two birds in the cage on the table, put a large cloth round it, switched out the light and before you could read the Kama Sutra, there was a shocking scuffle going on. She whipped her hand inside and grabbed the aggressive bird and said, 'So you must be the male. Now,' she went on, 'if I put you back in the cage I shan't know which you are, shall I?' So she tied a piece of white ribbon round its neck then put it back in the cage. Two days later the old vicar popped in for a chat. The bird took one look at his white collar and said, 'Oh, Gor Blimey, did they catch you at it as well?'

16.   It was an arid, dry, dusty, sleepy town in the Mid-West . . . real cowboy country, back in the good old days. Suddenly, a little cowboy ran through the dusty town shouting, 'Look out, everybody, Big John's coming!' A feeling of dread spread through the town and before he had finished the sentence the streets were cleared. Suddenly, from out of town there came the slap of leather, a ring of steel and the plodding of horses' hooves. Into view there came a giant 18-stone man, with shoulders like a bullock, sitting astride two horses. He pulled the horses up at the saloon, dismounted, took a horse's head in each hand and said, 'Wait here.' So saying, he banged their heads together and they both collapsed. He sauntered casually into the saloon, where the bar-tender stood trembling with fright. With careful gait, the stranger walked up and said, 'Gimme a whisky.' The barman, shaking all over, said, 'Whisky sir, yessir, right away, sir,' and so saying, handed him a whole bottle of whisky. The stranger took the bottle in one hand, ripped the cork out with his teeth and devoured the whole bottle. The little bar-tender looked up and said, 'Have another?' Whereupon the stranger said, 'Nope. I can't stay. BIG JOHN'S COMING.'

IN CONCLUSION

Well there they are, jokes, quotes and anecdotes, which I hope will be of some service to you when twisted to suit your own requirements.

They do say that brevity is the soul of wit and whereas I heartily concur with this, it is important that you draw the verbal picture as graphically as you can, for the more vivid and real your characters are, the more the interest is sustained and the more believable your stories.

The only thing one is not able to do is to teach somebody the essence of timing. This will naturally come with experience. If you draw a story out too long it will begin to pall before you get to the tag line, so draw your picture verbally only as long as it is necessary that the salient points are told, and then deliver the tag line, just before they are expecting it.

If you can imagine the action of chopping wood —your left hand is the audience and you hold them steady. The wood is your story, you poise it carefully and as soon as it is in position you deliver the chopper —which is your tag line.

I can only hope that somewhere between these lines you have found something to enable to you deliver many devastating blows and in conclusion I raise my glass to YOU, the next speaker.